Baking with Kim-Joy

Cute and Creative Bakes to Make You Smile

PHOTOGRAPHY BY ELLIS PARRINDER
ILLUSTRATIONS BY LINDA VAN DEN BERG
LETTERING DESIGN BY MARY KATE McDEVITT

Hardie Grant

QUADRILLE

Contents

Introduction

Baking is something that many of us associate with happy memories, joy and spending time with loved ones, so I wanted that to be reflected in this book through lots of colour and positive messages. I hope you will look through the book, relax with a cup of tea and escape from the world for a while, then get baking and, most importantly, ENJOY it.

I love decorating and creating stories within my bakes, so you will find that every recipe has some kind of decoration to it! I like to create bakes that you can attach a personality to, because I love the stories that people create around them. A lot of my inspiration comes from stories and, of course, animals! For instance, I might think of some delicious choux bun fillings, but then I also think about how I can make them have life and character, so I imagine different animals and how to make them work with the choux pastry. I live in my head a lot of the time, so I love things that are colourful, different and fantastical. I'm also inspired by my mistakes. Some of the bakes I have been most happy with have been born out of blunders, so I want to encourage mistakes and not try to make everything perfect. There are a few recipes, techniques and ideas in this book that, in particular, allow for slip-ups and encourage unpredictability in decorating, such as making coral (see pages 56–58), the Halloween Cake with Meringue Ghosts (see page 32), the Pigfiteroles in Mud (see page 166), Meringues (see page 152) and the abstract cookie and macaron painting on pages 82 and 122.

If you are a beginner baker, not confident with decorating yet or are short on time (because life can just take over), there are options to simplify any of the recipes. The tiered cakes on pages 12–31, for example, can be made and presented very simply and effectively, or they can be decorated with your favourite theme chosen from pages 32–59. You can also omit the decoration from the Breads (see pages 86–99) and Square Cakes (see pages 102–111), and the Little Bakes section (see pages 114–170) is filled with shorter bakes to try. There are clear step-by-step photos where necessary to help guide you.

Regardless of whether you are a beginner baker or more experienced, the two most important things about baking are: that you do what you love and do what is achievable one step at a time. If you enjoy decorating tiered cakes, start with getting the cake bases right, then work on the crumb coating, then move on to more complicated decorating techniques. It's never going to be perfect the first time and you will learn from your slip-ups (and occasionally create something wonderful from those mistakes!), but keep building your knowledge in a particular area before moving on to the next.

There's a lot of stress in our daily lives, so I hope this book can be a little place of calm away from all the hustle and bustle.

BAKE, BE ADVENTUROUS AND, ABOVE ALL, BE HAPPY!

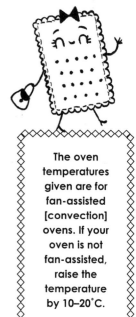

The oven temperatures given are for fan-assisted (convection) ovens. If your oven is not fan-assisted, raise the temperature by 10–20°C.

Some things you might not know about me

- I was born in Belgium. My mum is Chinese and originally from Malaysia, and my dad is English. I spoke French and English as a child, but forgot the French when I came to the UK aged five.

- My dad wanted to call me names such as 'Kimberley' and 'Katherine', which my mum thought were all too girly. Suddenly one day my mum said 'Kim-Joy, tomboy!' and the name stuck.

- I'm the middle child and have two brothers called Kenneth and Kevan. All our names start with the letter 'K'! I'm not sure why. I also have a half-sister called Crystal (if only it was spelled with a 'K' instead!) and a half-brother called Julian.

- I grew up on fighting games and Final Fantasy, as well as Sailor Moon, Dragon Ball Z and Cardcaptors. My brothers and I used to craft swords and bows out of tree branches, create imaginary characters, turn the house into an amusement park with dedicated areas for different rides (and a map!) and create forts out of mattresses to battle in.

- I probably was a bit of a tomboy, but I always liked dresses and colour – apart from going through a phase of wearing black as a teenager... though I quickly snapped out of that!

- No one in my family bakes. I just started baking as a hobby because it was a fun, creative outlet and made people happy.

- I never wear shoes unless I really have to. And definitely never when baking! I also do a lot of my decorating sitting on the floor.

- My background has always been in caring roles. I've worked as a care assistant in an elderly people's home, a support worker for people with learning disabilities and a mental health support worker in universities. I have always baked in my spare time, though more in certain periods of my life than in others!

- My favourite colour is yellow.

Though I love cats, I don't actually own one – or any pets! (I do have a sourdough starter called Sauron and he's lived with me for three years.)

Cakes & Frosting

Pistachio & Cardamom Cake with Mango-Saffron Jam

These are some of my favourite flavours all combined in one cake. Not only does the flavour shine through, the lovely thing about this cake is that it is wonderfully moist (thanks to the yoghurt/sour cream), while also being light and fluffy due to the technique of folding in the whisked egg whites. This cake has a natural and subtle colour from the pistachio, which contrasts nicely with the mango jam oozing out from the buttercream layers.

SERVES: 20–25 (MAKES 4 X 18-CM [7-IN] CAKES)

MANGO-SAFFRON JAM
250g [8¾oz] mango (preferably semi-ripe), peeled and roughly chopped
250g [1¼ cups] jam sugar
3–5 cardamom pods
a small pinch of saffron threads, or to taste

MIXTURE A
180g [1⅓ cups] roasted, unsalted and shelled pistachios
2 tsp ground cardamom (for the best flavour, finely grind the seeds in a spice grinder)
480g [3⅔ cups] self-raising [self-rising] flour
1¼ tsp baking powder
300ml [1¼ cups] whole milk
145g [⅔ cup] whole yoghurt or sour cream
270g [1¼ cups] unsalted butter, at room temperature, plus extra for greasing
390g [2 cups] caster or granulated sugar
½ tsp salt
1 large egg
1 tsp vanilla bean paste
1 tsp almond extract

MIXTURE B
3 large egg whites
¼ tsp cream of tartar

PLUS
1 quantity of Italian Meringue Buttercream (see page 64) or American Buttercream (see page 60), flavoured with 1 Tbsp vanilla bean paste
extra pistachios, crushed

1 / First, make the mango-saffron jam. Cook the mango in a pan over a low heat for 2 minutes, or until the juices start releasing. Add the sugar and cardamom pods, and stir every so often until the sugar has completely dissolved, then bring the mixture to a rapid rolling boil for about 5–10 minutes. Stir regularly to make sure it doesn't burn on the bottom. When the jam has reached 105°C [221°F], it is ready. Add the saffron to taste, then decant into a jar or bowl, cover and leave to cool to room temperature before using.

2 / Preheat the oven to 180°C [350°F/Gas mark 4]. Grease 4 x 18-cm [7-in] cake tins and line the bases with baking paper.

Watch out! This produces quite a bit of mix, so you will need a large mixing bowl to fold in the egg whites!

3 / For Mixture A, add the pistachios to a food processor and process until they resemble fine crumbs. Mix with the ground cardamom, flour and baking powder.

4 / In separate bowl, mix the milk and yoghurt or sour cream together. Set aside.

5 / Place the butter, sugar and salt in a stand mixer (or use a handheld electric whisk) fitted with a balloon whisk attachment and whisk on medium speed until the butter is smooth, then whisk on high

until pale in colour, soft and fluffy. Occasionally scrape down the sides of the bowl so that everything mixes evenly.

6 / Add the egg and mix until well combined, then add the vanilla bean paste and almond extract and mix again.

7 / Add the flour mixture and milk mixture alternately, mixing on slow until just combined. Set aside.

8 / For Mixture B, add the egg whites to a clean stand mixer (or use a clean handheld electric whisk) and whisk on high speed until soft peaks form. Add the cream of tartar and continue whisking until stiff peaks form.

9 / Now fold the beaten egg whites into Mixture A, one-third at a time. Divide the mixture evenly among the prepared cake tins and bake for 30–40 minutes until a knife inserted into the centre comes out clean.

10 / Leave to cool in the tins for 5 minutes, then run a knife around the edges of the cakes and flip onto a rack. Peel off the baking paper.

11 / While the cakes are cooling, make your choice of buttercream (see pages 64 or 60), flavouring it with the vanilla bean paste. Transfer the buttercream to a large piping [pastry] bag and snip a large tip.

12 / Make sure the cakes and jam are cool before assembling. Stack the cakes using the guide on page 68. In between each cake layer, pipe an even layer of buttercream and smooth with a palette knife, then pipe a dam (see pages 68–69) and spoon in a generous amount of jam. Continue until you have 3 layers of buttercream and jam and have placed the fourth cake layer on top. Cover the top and sides with buttercream and smooth (if this works with your chosen cake design). Chill in the fridge, or freezer if you're in a rush.

This cake will look and taste beautiful if it's kept simple with just some crushed pistachios scattered on top and some edible flowers, or use it with any of the decorating themes!

Make a dark chocolate ganache (see opposite) instead of a buttercream here and you could use this cake base for the Woodland Cake (see page 46).

Vegan Chocolate Cake with Praline

Yes, this is a vegan cake, but don't let that fool you into thinking that this isn't extremely fluffy, moist and decadently chocolatey. It's a chocolate cake of dreams and no one will be able to tell it's vegan! The ganache with coconut milk tastes exactly like ganache made with cream – there is no trace of a coconut flavour because the dark chocolate completely overpowers it. And the addition of praline paste in the filling just adds that extra nutty depth of flavour to make you want to really savour your slice of this cake. Yummyyyyyy.

SERVES: 16–20 (MAKES 3 X 18-CM [7-IN] CAKES)

600ml [2½ cups] soy milk
2¼ tsp white wine vinegar
135g [⅓ cup plus 1 Tbsp] golden [light corn] syrup
225ml [1 cup] sunflower oil or other neutral-tasting oil, plus extra for oiling
420g [3 cups plus 4 tsp] self-raising [self-rising] flour
315g [1½ cups] caster or granulated sugar

75g [¾ cup] cocoa powder
3 tsp baking powder
¾ tsp bicarbonate of soda [baking soda]

PRALINE PASTE
130g [⅔ cup] caster [superfine] sugar
35ml [2⅓ Tbsp] water
1 tsp liquid glucose, to help prevent the mixture crystallizing (optional)

75g [½ cup] hazelnuts, toasted in a dry pan over a low-medium heat for a few minutes

VEGAN GANACHE
400g [14oz] vegan dark chocolate, chopped into small pieces
300ml [1¼ cups] coconut milk

100–250g [¾ cup minus ½ Tbsp–1¾ cups] icing [confectioners'] sugar (depends on chocolate brand and desired level of sweetness)

OPTIONAL
100g [¾ cup] cacao nibs (add this to the batter before baking for extra flavour)

1 / Preheat the oven to 170°C [340°F/Gas mark 3]. Oil the base and sides of 3 x 18-cm [7-in] cake tins and line the bases with baking paper.

2 / Whisk the soy milk and vinegar together in a large bowl. Leave to curdle and thicken (this should happen in seconds).

3 / Place the golden syrup in a small bowl and microwave until liquid. Add the oil and golden syrup to the curdled milk and whisk to combine. It will separate but that's OK.

4 / In a separate large bowl, mix together all the remaining dry ingredients with the cacao nibs at this

point, if using. Use a sieve for the cocoa powder to distribute it evenly without clumps.

5 / Add the dry ingredients to the wet ingredients and, using a balloon whisk, whisk until just combined. Be careful not to overwhisk. Divide the batter evenly between the prepared cake tins and bake for about 30 minutes, or until a knife inserted into the centre comes out clean.

6 / While the cakes are baking, make the praline paste. Add the sugar, water and liquid glucose, if using, to a pan. Stir to combine, then bring to the boil and stop stirring. This is very important – if you stir, then the mixture will crystallize. Meanwhile, place

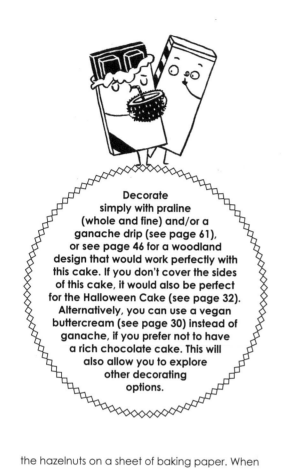

Decorate simply with praline (whole and fine) and/or a ganache drip (see page 61), or see page 46 for a woodland design that would work perfectly with this cake. If you don't cover the sides of this cake, it would also be perfect for the Halloween Cake (see page 32). Alternatively, you can use a vegan buttercream (see page 30) instead of ganache, if you prefer not to have a rich chocolate cake. This will also allow you to explore other decorating options.

the hazelnuts on a sheet of baking paper. When the mixture turns medium amber, pour it over the hazelnuts and leave to set. Set aside a few whole pieces of set praline to decorate, if liked. Place the remainder in a food processor and blitz until it becomes a paste. Set aside.

7 / When the cakes are baked, run a knife around the edges and turn out onto racks. Peel off the baking paper and leave to cool.

8 / Meanwhile, make the vegan ganache. Place the chocolate in a large heatproof bowl. Heat the coconut milk in a pan until just starting to bubble, then pour onto the chocolate. Leave for 2 minutes, then stir until all the chocolate has melted. If there are still pieces of unmelted chocolate, transfer to a pan and stir over a low heat until all the chocolate has melted.

9 / Use a spatula to transfer the chocolate to a stand mixer (or use a handheld electric whisk) fitted with a balloon whisk attachment, add the sugar and whisk until just combined. Transfer two-thirds of the

ganache to a bowl. Cover with plastic wrap (make sure it touches the surface to avoid a skin forming) and chill in the fridge for 10–15 minutes. This will be for covering the sides of the cake.

10 / Add the praline paste to the remaining third of the ganache and whisk until light in colour and thickened to a firm but still spreadable consistency. This will be used for filling in between the cake layers.

11 / Make sure the cakes are cool before assembling. Stack the cakes using the guide on page 68. If the ganache is too cold, it will be too firm to spread, and if it is too warm, it will be too runny. You can adjust this by heating and cooling the ganache to get the right consistency. In between each cake layer, spread an even layer of praline ganache using a palette knife. Continue until you have 2 layers of ganache and have placed the third layer on top. Cover the top and sides with the ganache from the fridge and smooth. Refrigerate until ready to serve.

Lemon, Rose & Raspberry Cake

This cake is your classic buttery sponge that everyone loves! The flavours are complementary and will definitely leave you wanting another slice, so be warned.

SERVES: 20–25 (MAKES 4 X 18-CM [7-IN] CAKES)

345g [1½ cups] unsalted butter, at room temperature, cubed, plus extra for greasing

345g [1¾ cups] caster or granulated sugar

½ tsp salt

345g [12oz] shelled eggs (about 5 large)

grated zest of 3 large lemons

1 tsp vanilla bean paste

500g [3¾ cups] self-raising [self-rising] flour

LEMON SIMPLE SYRUP

240ml [1 cup] freshly squeezed lemon juice

240g [1¼ cups] caster or granulated sugar

PLUS

1 quantity of Italian Meringue (see page 64) or American Buttercream (see page 60), with 1½–2½ Tbsp rosewater to flavour (taste, as the flavour intensity can vary between different brands)

250g or 1 punnet [2 cups] raspberries

1 / Preheat the oven to 170°C [340°F/Gas mark 3]. Grease 4 x 18-cm [7-in] cake tins and line the bases with baking paper.

2 / Place the butter, sugar and salt in a stand mixer (or use a handheld electric whisk) fitted with a balloon whisk attachment and beat on medium speed until the butter is smooth, then increase the speed to high and beat until the butter is fluffy and pale in colour.

3 / Lightly beat the eggs in a separate bowl. Add the eggs, 1 Tbsp at a time, to the creamed butter and sugar mixture, beating well after each addition. Add the lemon zest and vanilla bean paste and mix to combine.

4 / Sift in half the flour and mix on low speed to combine. Then sift in the remaining flour and continue mixing on low until just combined.

5 / Divide the batter among the prepared cake tins and bake for 30–40 minutes until a knife inserted into the centre comes out clean.

6 / For the lemon simple syrup, heat all the ingredients together in a pan over a medium heat, stirring occasionally, until the mixture comes to a simmer. Simmer for 3 minutes, then take off the heat.

7 / When the cakes are baked, leave them in their tins for 5 minutes, then run a knife around the edges and turn them out onto racks. Peel off the baking paper. Immediately poke holes all over the cakes and use a pastry brush to soak both sides of the sponges with the lemon syrup. Leave to cool.

8 / Meanwhile, make your choice of buttercream (see pages 64 or 60) and flavour with rosewater to taste. Add the rosewater gradually to avoid the buttercream splitting. Transfer the buttercream to a large piping [pastry] bag and snip a large tip.

9 / Make sure the cakes are cool before assembling. Stack them using the guide on page 68. In between each cake layer and on top of the cake, pipe an even layer of buttercream and smooth with a palette knife, then add raspberries in the centre. If you want, try any of the decorating themes on pages 32–59!

- CAKES & FROSTING -

Ginger, Pecan & Salted Caramel Cake

The ginger flavour of this cake comes from both ground ginger and stem ginger, so there is a strong ginger undercurrent, and as a bonus you occasionally get a burst from a chunk of stem ginger. The pecans and salted caramel complement it perfectly – you will definitely want to go back for seconds.

SERVES: 16–20 (MAKES 3 X 18-CM [7-IN] CAKES)

250g [1 cup plus 2 Tbsp] unsalted butter, plus extra for greasing
¼ tsp salt
250g [1¼ cups] dark muscovado [soft brown] sugar
120g [⅓ cup] black treacle [molasses]

375g [2¾ cups plus 1½ Tbsp] self-raising [self-rising] flour
4 Tbsp ground ginger
1 Tbsp ground cinnamon
300ml [1¼ cups] whole milk
100g [3½oz] crystallized stem [candied preserved] ginger, finely chopped

3 large eggs
2 tsp bicarbonate of soda [baking soda]

SALTED CARAMEL
90ml [6 Tbsp] water
240g [1¼ cups] caster or granulated sugar
225ml [1 cup] double [heavy] cream
salt, to taste

PLUS
1 quantity of Cream Cheese Frosting (see page 60)
120g [1 cup] pecans, lightly toasted and roughly chopped

1 / Preheat the oven to 180°C [350°F/Gas mark 4]. Grease 3 x 18-cm [7-in] cake tins and line the bases with baking paper.

2 / For the cake, heat the butter, salt, muscovado sugar and treacle in a small pan over a low-medium heat, stirring constantly, until the butter has melted and combined.

3 / Combine the flour and ground spices in a separate bowl.

4 / Heat the milk in a small bowl in the microwave for a minute until warm. Set aside.

5 / Pour the liquid sugar and butter mixture over the flour mixture, then stir quickly until smooth and combined. Add the chopped ginger, then the eggs, one at a time, mixing well after each addition.

6 / Add the bicarbonate of soda to the reserved warm milk and mix until foamy. Pour this into the main mixture and mix with a balloon whisk until smooth and just combined. Immediately pour the mixture evenly between the prepared cake tins and bake for 25–35 minutes until a knife inserted into the centre comes out clean.

7 / While the cake is baking, make the salted caramel. Heat the water and sugar in a saucepan over a low-medium heat, stirring occasionally, until the sugar has completely dissolved. Once the sugar has dissolved, turn up the heat and wait (don't stir) until the sugar turns an amber colour. You can swill the pan around to even out the colour.

8 / When the sugar syrup has turned a deep amber colour, remove the pan from the heat, add the cream in one go and stir constantly with a balloon whisk. The caramel will bubble up, so be careful

at this stage! Return the pan to the stove over a low heat and continue stirring until all the sugar has dissolved and you have a smooth and creamy caramel. Pour into a medium bowl and sprinkle with a little salt to taste. Don't add too much; it's better to add too little than too much. Cover with plastic wrap and chill in the freezer for 30–45 minutes. It will thicken as it cools.

9 / When the cakes are baked, leave them to cool in their tins for 5 minutes, then run a knife around the edges and turn them out onto racks. Peel off the baking paper and leave to cool.

10 / Meanwhile, make the cream cheese frosting (see page 60), then transfer to a large piping [pastry] bag and cut a large tip.

11 / Make sure the cakes and caramel are cool before assembling. Stack the cakes using the guide on page 68. In between each cake layer, pipe the frosting, drizzle the caramel and sprinkle with a third of the pecans. Continue until you have 2 layers of frosting and caramel, and have placed the third cake layer on top. Pipe the frosting on top of the cake and smooth with a palette knife. Cover the sides with more frosting, or leave them naked, depending on how you are planning to decorate this cake. Chill in the fridge, or freezer if you're in a rush. Then it's time to decorate!

This cake would be perfect as a Halloween theme cake (see page 32), Easter cake (see page 50), Christmas cake (see page 38) or even a woodland cake (see page 46). However, the cream cheese frosting is not advisable for coloured buttercream cakes, as it doesn't set as hard as buttercream does!

Spiced Carrot & Walnut Cake

Carrot cake is the kind of treat that is a favourite all year round. You can pretend it's good for you because it contains a lot of carrots, but really it is way too tasty to be that healthy! I love this recipe because it's fluffy, decadent and moist, and the raisins and walnuts add texture and flavour so that you absolutely *wal nut* be able to resist this!

SERVES: 16–20 (MAKES 3 X 18-CM [7-IN] CAKES)

unsalted butter, for
  greasing
275g [2 cups] plain
  [all-purpose] flour
2 tsp baking powder
3½ tsp ground cinnamon
2½ tsp ground ginger
¼ tsp ground cloves

grated zest of 1 medium
  orange
310ml [1¼ cups]
  vegetable oil
425g [2 cups plus 2 Tbsp]
  light muscovado [soft
  brown] sugar
¼ tsp salt

1 tsp vanilla extract
255g [9oz] shelled eggs
  (about 5 medium)
320g [2⅓ cups] grated
  carrot
70g [½ cup] raisins
105g [1 cup] toasted
  walnuts, chopped

PLUS
1 quantity of Cream
  Cheese Frosting (see
  page 60)
1 quantity of Salted
  Caramel (see page 20),
  optional

1 / Preheat the oven to 170°C [340°F/Gas mark 3]. Grease 3 x 18-cm [7-in] cake tins, and line the bases with baking paper.

2 / Mix the flour, baking powder, cinnamon, ginger, cloves and orange zest together in a bowl.

3 / Add the oil, muscovado sugar, salt and vanilla to a stand mixer (or use a handheld electric whisk) fitted with a balloon whisk attachment and mix on high speed until there are no sugar lumps left. Add the eggs, one by one, beating well after each addition.

4 / With the mixer on low, add the dry ingredients to the wet, adding a third at a time.

5 / Fold in the carrot, raisins and walnuts by hand, then pour the batter into the prepared cake tins. Bake for 35–40 minutes until a knife inserted into the centre of the cake comes out clean and the cakes have shrunk away from the edges of the tins slightly.

6 / When the cakes are baked, leave them to cool in the tins for 5 minutes, then run a knife around the edges and turn out onto racks. Peel off the baking paper and leave to cool.

7 / Meanwhile, make the cream cheese frosting (see page 60), then transfer to a large piping [pastry] bag and cut a large tip.

8 / Make sure the cakes and caramel, if using, are cool before assembling. Stack the cakes using the guide on page 68. In between each cake layer, pipe the frosting and drizzle the caramel sauce, if using. Continue until you have 2 layers of frosting and caramel, if using, and have placed the third cake layer on top. Pipe the frosting on top of the cake. Cover the sides with more frosting, or leave them naked, depending on how you are planning to decorate this cake. Chill in the fridge, or freezer if you're in a rush. Then it's time to decorate!

Blueberry Cake with Orange Curd

This cake is beautifully light, with occasional welcome bursts of blueberry. It is delicious paired with the slight acidity from the orange curd. Make sure you use dowels if stacking this cake, as it is on the delicate side.

SERVES: 20–25 (MAKES 4 X 18-CM [7-IN] CAKES)

MIXTURE A
335g [1½ cups] unsalted butter, at room temperature, cubed, plus extra for greasing
300g [1½ cups] caster or granulated sugar
½ tsp salt

6 medium egg yolks
2 tsp vanilla bean paste
495g [3⅔ cups] self-raising [self-rising] flour, plus extra for coating the blueberries
240ml [1 cup] whole milk
420g [3⅓ cups] blueberries

MIXTURE B
6 medium egg whites
150g [¾ cup] caster or granulated sugar

PLUS
1 quantity of Italian Meringue Buttercream (see page 64) or American Buttercream (see page 60)
1 quantity of Orange Curd (see page 62)

1 / Preheat the oven to 190°C [375°F/Gas mark 5]. Grease 4 x 18-cm [7-in] cake tins and line the bases with baking paper.

2 / First, prepare Mixture A. Place the butter, sugar and salt in a stand mixer (or use a handheld electric whisk) fitted with a balloon whisk attachment and whisk on medium speed until the butter is smooth. Increase the speed to high and whisk until it is pale in colour, soft and fluffy. Occasionally scrape down the sides of the bowl so that it mixes evenly.

3 / Add the egg yolks, one at a time, beating well after each addition, then add the vanilla bean paste. Add the flour and milk alternately, mixing on slow until it is just combined. Set aside.

4 / For Mixture B, add the egg whites to a clean stand mixer (or use a clean handheld electric whisk) and whisk on high speed until soft peaks form, then gradually add the sugar, 1 Tbsp at a time, whisking constantly. When all the sugar has been mixed in, fold the egg whites into Mixture A, a third at a time.

5 / Coat the blueberries in flour, then fold them into the batter. Divide the batter evenly between the prepared cake tins and bake for 40–50 minutes until a knife inserted into the centre comes out clean.

6 / Leave the cakes to cool in the tins for 5 minutes, then run a knife around the edges and turn out onto racks. Peel off the paper and leave to cool.

7 / While the cakes are cooling, make your choice of buttercream (see pages 64 or 60). You can flavour the buttercream with lemon zest to make an extra fruity cake – blueberry, lemon and orange! Transfer the buttercream to a large [pastry] piping bag.

8 / Make sure the cakes and curd are cool before assembling. Start to stack the cakes – in between each cake layer, pipe an even layer of buttercream and smooth with a palette knife, then spoon over a third of the orange curd. Continue until you have 3 layers of buttercream and curd and have placed the fourth layer on top. Chill in the fridge, or freezer if you're in a rush. Then it's time to decorate, if liked!

Orange & Amaretto Rainbow Cake

Delicious flavours and a rainbow cake – how can you say no to that? Plus you can fill this with loads of sweets for a fun piñata-style reveal that kids will love! You can make all six cakes at once if you feel confident managing a large amount of mixture (the batter will just about fit in a stand mixer) and baking six cakes at the same time. If not, then just split the recipe in half and make three cakes at a time.

SERVES: 30–40 (MAKES 6 X 18-CM [7-IN] CAKES)

525g [2⅓ cups] unsalted butter, plus extra for greasing
525g [2⅔ cups] caster or granulated sugar
¾ tsp salt
525g [18½oz] shelled eggs (about 8 large)
grated zest of 6 oranges

1½ tsp vanilla bean paste
600g [4½ cups] self-raising [self-rising] flour
150g [1½ cups] finely ground almonds
purple, blue, green, yellow, orange and red food dyes

ORANGE & AMARETTO SIMPLE SYRUP
360ml [1½ cups] freshly squeezed orange juice
300g [1½ cups] caster or granulated sugar
4 Tbsp amaretto

PLUS
1 quantity of Italian Meringue Buttercream (see page 64) or American Buttercream (see page 60), flavoured with 2–2½ tsp almond extract
sweets [candies], to fill the centre of the cake

1 / Preheat the oven to 170°C [340°F/Gas mark 3]. Grease 6 x 18-cm [7-in] cake tins and line the bases with baking paper.

2 / Place the butter, sugar and salt in a stand mixer (or use a handheld electric whisk) fitted with a balloon whisk attachment and beat on medium speed until the butter is smooth. Increase the speed and beat on high until the butter is fluffy and pale in colour.

3 / Lightly beat the eggs in a separate bowl, then add the eggs, 1 Tbsp at a time, to the creamed butter and sugar mixture, beating well after each addition. Add the orange zest and vanilla bean paste and mix to combine.

4 / Sift a third of the flour in at a time, mixing on low speed after each addition to combine. Add the ground almonds and continue mixing on low speed until just combined.

5 / Divide the batter evenly among 6 bowls (you can use weighing scales to ensure each layer is equal). Add the food dye and mix to create 6 different colours: purple, blue, green, yellow, orange and red (do 3 colours if you are making half the recipe at a time).

6 / Transfer each coloured bowl of batter to a prepared cake tin and bake for 30–40 minutes until a knife inserted into the centre comes out clean.

7 / Meanwhile, make the orange & amaretto simple syrup. Heat the orange juice and sugar in a small pan over a medium-high heat, stirring occasionally, until the mixture comes to a simmer. Simmer for 3 minutes, then take off the heat. Transfer to a bowl and leave to cool, before stirring in the amaretto.

8 / When the cakes are baked, leave them in their tins for 5 minutes, then run a knife around the edges and turn out onto racks. Peel off the paper.

STEP 12 ▲

9 / Immediately poke holes all over the cakes and use a pastry brush to soak both sides of the sponges with the syrup. Try to distribute the syrup evenly over all the sponges. Leave to cool.

10 / Meanwhile, make your choice of buttercream (see pages 64 or 60) and flavour with the almond extract, to taste. Transfer the buttercream to a large piping [pastry] bag and snip a large tip.

11 / Make sure the cakes are cool before assembling. First, use a small round cutter (mine is 5.5cm [2¼in])
to cut out holes in the centre of each cake – apart from the red cake, as this will go on top.

You can eat these cutouts straightaway or stack them together to make a mini cake!

12 / Stack the cakes using the guide on page 68. In between each cake layer, pipe an even layer of buttercream and smooth with a palette knife, but

don't cover up the hole. Stack the cakes in rainbow order: purple, blue, green, yellow, orange, then red. Before placing the final red cake layer on top, throw all the sweets down the central hole of the cake.

13 / Place the red layer on top, cover the top and sides (if required for your chosen cake design) with buttercream and smooth. Chill in the fridge, or freezer if you're in a rush, before decorating.

This cake would be perfect for a celebration, as it's so fun when you cut a slice and all the sweets pour out! It would also be perfect for the All-the-Colour Cake on page 34 (rainbows on the inside AND outside!), as well as the Cat Paradise Cake (see page 54) because it sets in the clouds, but you can also make it work with any of the other cake decorating themes. For example, the rainbow reveal would be an unexpected and interesting contrast to the Halloween Cake (see page 32), and the addition of salted caramel would complement this cake! There are no rules.

- CAKES & FROSTING -

Vegan Vanilla Cake with Lemon Curd & Blackberries

This fluffy cake is loved by vegans and non-vegans alike, and pairs beautifully with the sharp lemon curd. The best thing is how quick it is to make the mixture, with no need for a stand mixer – two bowls, your cake tins, spoons and a balloon whisk are all you will have to wash up. The reaction between the acidity in the wet ingredients and the baking powder makes this cake rise, so once the wet and dry ingredients are mixed, it is all about getting this cake into the oven as quickly as possible! And then getting to enjoy it as quickly as possible!

SERVES: 20–24 (MAKES 4 X 18-CM [7-IN] CAKES)

WET INGREDIENTS
2½ tsp white wine vinegar
560ml [2⅓ cups] soy milk
225ml [1 cup] sunflower oil or other neutral-tasting oil, plus extra for oiling
1¾ Tbsp liquid from a can of chickpeas [garbanzo beans], i.e. aquafaba
1 Tbsp vanilla bean paste
½ tsp salt

DRY INGREDIENTS
500g [3¾ cups] self-raising [self-rising] flour
375g [2 cups minus 2 Tbsp] caster or granulated sugar
1¾ Tbsp baking powder

VEGAN LEMON CURD
200ml [¾ cup] lemon juice (juice of 4–5 lemons)
grated zest of 4 lemons
240g [1¼ cups] caster or granulated sugar
2 Tbsp arrowroot powder or cornflour [cornstarch]
80g [⅓ cup] coconut oil
60ml [¼ cup] coconut milk

VEGAN VANILLA BUTTERCREAM
200g [¾ cup plus 2 Tbsp] vegetarian margarine block, cubed
500g [2½ cups] vegetable shortening
770g [5½ cups] icing [confectioners'] sugar

PLUS
1 punnet blackberries, or other fresh fruit

OPTIONAL
add the grated zest of 3 lemons to the dry cake ingredients for an extra lemon zing, or 1⅓ Tbsp culinary lavender buds (grind in a mortar and pestle first to soften and bring out the flavour) for a lavender and lemon cake

1 / Preheat the oven to 170°C [340°F/Gas mark 3]. Oil 4 x 18-cm [7-in] cake tins and line the bases with baking paper.

2 / For the wet ingredients, mix the vinegar with the soy milk in a large bowl until it curdles and thickens. Mix in the remaining wet ingredients.

3 / In a separate large bowl, combine all the dry ingredients.

4 / Add the dry ingredients to the wet and whisk until just combined. Pour the batter straightaway into the prepared tins and bake for 25–30 minutes until a knife inserted into the centre comes out clean and they are springy to the touch.

5 / Meanwhile, make the vegan lemon curd. Combine the lemon juice, zest, sugar and arrowroot or cornflour in a small pan. Stir constantly over a medium heat until it thickens and coats the back of a spoon. Take off the heat, then immediately add the coconut oil with the milk and stir in until it is completely melted and combined. Pour into a bowl and cover with plastic wrap (making sure it touches the surface to avoid a film forming). Chill in the

freezer for 1 hour. It won't seem very thick right now, but will thicken to the perfect consistency as it cools.

This lemon curd is the star of the cake, as you can't tell it is vegan at all! It contains coconut milk and oil, but the flavour of the lemon is so strong that it masks the coconut. I like my lemon curd on the tart side when it's going to be sandwiched between sweet buttercream and cake, but if you want it sweeter, then add 2–3 more Tbsp of sugar, to taste.

6 / When the cakes are baked, run a knife around the edges, then turn out onto racks. Peel off the baking paper and leave to cool.

7 / Meanwhile, make the buttercream. Place the margarine in a stand mixer (or use a handheld electric whisk) fitted with a balloon whisk attachment and mix on low-medium speed until smooth. Add the vegetable shortening and icing sugar and continue mixing until smooth and combined. Whisk until fluffy, but do not overwhisk, as the vegetable shortening can very easily split and become grainy. If this happens, you can still use the buttercream. I prefer it smooth, but some people quite like it grainy.

8 / Transfer some of the buttercream to a large piping [pastry] bag and snip a large tip.

9 / Make sure the cakes and curd are cool before assembling. Stack the cakes using the guide on page 68. In between each cake layer, pipe an even layer of buttercream and smooth with a palette knife, then pipe a dam (see pages 68–69) and spoon in a third of the lemon curd. Add blackberries or your chosen fruit in the centres between each layer. Continue until you have 3 layers of buttercream, curd and fruit, and you have placed the fourth cake layer on top. Crumb-coat the top and sides with buttercream and smooth if desired for a decorating theme (see pages 68–69). Chill in the freezer before decorating – this will make the vegan buttercream much firmer than if you put it in the fridge.

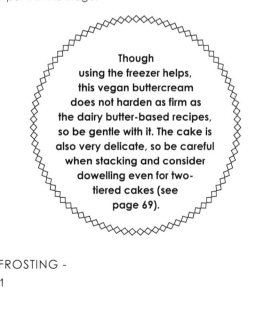

Though using the freezer helps, this vegan buttercream does not harden as firm as the dairy butter-based recipes, so be gentle with it. The cake is also very delicate, so be careful when stacking and consider dowelling even for two-tiered cakes (see page 69).

Halloween Cake with Meringue Ghosts

Ideally, use the Spiced Carrot & Walnut Cake or Ginger, Pecan & Salted Caramel Cake (see pages 22 or 20) for this. If you have time, do make the little gingerbread house, poached pears and meringue ghosts. This is a great cake to do with kids, as everyone can decorate their own ghosts! Try making ghosts to represent each other. Maybe some are peaceful and others are vengeful spirits? The best thing about Halloween baking is that it doesn't have to be neat. Wonky, cracked meringues have personality; imperfect houses look perfectly planned to give them that abandoned look; who can say how a spooky pear should look.

SERVES: 20–24

POACHED PEARS
spices, such as 1 whole
   clove, 4 cardamom
   pods, 1 cinnamon stick,
   1 tsp vanilla bean paste
1 tsp dark brown sugar
3 pears

MERINGUE GHOSTS
1 quantity of Meringue
   mixture (see page 150)

GINGERBREAD HOUSE
1 quantity of Ginger
   Cookie dough (see page
   74)
1 quantity of Royal Icing
   (see page 76)

PLUS
black and red food dye
a cake from pages 12–31,
   baked and cooled
a filling from pages 60–65
Salted Caramel (see page
   20)

1 / For the poached pears, place a pan of water on the stove and bring to the boil, then add all the spices and the sugar. Peel the pears, leaving the stems intact, and slice off the bottoms. Put them into the water to simmer for 20–30 minutes until soft.

2 / Meanwhile, make the meringue and pipe into a variety of ghosts, then bake (see pages 150–152).

3 / Now make the ginger cookie dough (see page 74), roll out and cut out the right shapes (you can find templates online). Bake, then cool on a rack.

4 / Make the royal icing and dye a small amount black (see page 76). Put into separate piping bags.

5 / When the pears are soft, take them out of the water and leave to drain on a clean tea [dish] towel.

6 / To assemble the house, use royal icing to line up the sides, then place the roof on top last. Pipe spooky details, such as ghosts and angry faces.

7 / Using black food dye, pipe or paint faces onto the meringue ghosts. Carve faces into the pears and use a brush to add 'gore' with red and black dye.

8 / Assemble your cake layers with your chosen filling.

9 / Now for the fun part! Carefully control some drips of salted caramel down the sides of the cake (see page 61). Position the house with the haunted pears just behind. Assemble meringue ghosts on top of the cake and wedged into the buttercream down the sides. Splatter red food dye as desired. (I sometimes get too enthusiastic about this and the kitchen becomes covered, but it's oh-so-satisfying…)

All-the-Colour Cake

Use any American or Italian meringue buttercream-based recipe for this cake, but just avoid using dark chocolate ganache, as well as the cream cheese frosting, as they are harder to work with in this way. The Orange & Amaretto Rainbow Cake (see page 26) works perfectly with this cake, as there will be colour on the outside AND the inside!

This cake is for those days where you just want to express yourself with colour and texture in an abstract way. A bit of texture is a GOOD thing here, so don't worry about making the cake super smooth. Anything you do is 'intended' – YOU are the artist.

As usual, all the decorations can be vegan, but just make sure you choose vegan food dyes.

SERVES: 30–40

CHOCOLATE SAIL
500g [18oz] good-quality white chocolate (no vegetable oils), finely chopped
OR
300g [10½oz] white compound chocolate (quicker and easier, looks just as good but isn't as tasty); you can also use vegan white chocolate
*There's a bigger quantity of white chocolate because it is easier to temper in larger quantities – leftovers can always be remelted

WHITE GANACHE DRIP
see page 61
white food dye (or metallic paint)

PLUS
a filling from pages 60 or 64–5
a cake from pages 12–30, baked and cooled
yellow, pink, white, pale blue, orange and dark blue food dyes

1 / Divide the buttercream (leftover from crumb-coating the cake, or make more, see pages 60 or 64–5, if required) among 6 bowls of colour: yellow, pink, white, pale blue, orange and dark blue.

Or pick your own colours!

2 / Working on the blank canvas (your crumb-coated cake), use an offset palette knife to smooth on different colours in different areas. Use a cake scraper to smooth certain areas, but then leave some lines raised and textured. Smooth the top edge using an offset spatula (see page 70).

> You can make this cake in a million different ways – it will never be exactly the same each time! Try working with colours on just the top half of the cake, or just the middle section, or even just pops of colour here and there. Look at some of your favourite artwork or beautiful scenery for inspiration. There are lots of ways to do this!

3 / Chill the cake while you make the chocolate sail. See page 64 on how to temper your white chocolate, or skip this if using compound chocolate and simply melt in the microwave in 15–30-second bursts, stirring well after each burst. Pour a small amount of chocolate onto a sheet of baking paper (or a piece of acetate or a piping bag), then smooth thin with an offset spatula. Use pegs to hold the creases of the baking paper to create a wavy 'sail' and leave to set (see picture below). Once set, carefully peel the sail away from the baking paper, then use a sharp blade to smooth the edges.

Alternatively: You can paint the sail any metallic colour, or just leave it white with some edible sprinkles or other tasty condiments to match the inside of the cake (such as nuts).

4 / See page 61 to make the ganache for the white drips down the side of the cake. Colour the ganache white. If you don't have white food dye, you can paint the drips with metallic paint after they have set.

5 / Remove the cake from the fridge and use a spoon or piping bag to create a drip effect (see page 61). Position the sail on top.

STEP 3 ▼

Snowy Christmas Cake

This design works perfectly with any cake recipe that has a buttercream or cream cheese frosting. To create more of a nighttime Christmas scene, you can also use dark chocolate ganache. You can design this cake as a single-, double- or triple-tiered sprawling town – depending on how many people you need to feed!

As usual, all the decorations can be vegan.

SERVES: 20–24

CHRISTMAS HOUSES
choose a cookie recipe (see pages 74–75)
½ quantity of Royal Icing (see page 76)

CHRISTMAS TREES
Option 1: a fir tree mould, cornflour [cornstarch] and dark green sugarpaste

Option 2: Royal Icing (see page 76), dark green food dye, some cocktail sticks [toothpicks], edible festive sprinkles, such as stars and snowflakes (this needs time overnight to set)

Option 3: dark green compound chocolate, some cocktail sticks [toothpicks], edible festive sprinkles, such as stars and snowflakes

PLUS
a cake from pages 12–31, baked and cooled

a filling from pages 60–65
Salted Caramel (see page 20)
gold and silver edible paint (optional)
red sugarpaste icing [confectioners'] sugar, for dusting

1a / If using cream cheese frosting as your filling, just cover the top and sides of the cake and smooth, then chill in the fridge or freezer.

1b / If you are using buttercream, then this design is made for a rough-textured edge at the top of the cake. To do this, smooth over the second coat of buttercream, but don't blend in the top edge which naturally forms above the cake. You can leave the colour of this second layer white, or you can colour it blue, or you can do a watercolour effect of blue and white, like a cloudy sky (see page 70). Leave the cake to chill in the fridge or freezer until firm, then using a brush, paint the rim of the uneven top edge with edible gold paint (see picture on page 40).

No time? You can also just leave the cake semi-naked (just crumb-coat) for a more rustic feel.

2 / Make the Christmas houses. Choose a cookie recipe (see pages 74–75) and either use shaped cutters or go freehand to cut out your houses.

3 / Make the royal icing (see page 76) and pipe details onto the houses to give them character and feel lived in (see my piping tips on pages 78–81.

4a / To make Christmas trees: Option 1. Dust your fir tree mould with cornflour, then firmly press the green sugarpaste into all the grooves and smooth the back (see picture on page 40). Turn the mould upside down and slowly and carefully peel away the mould. Try lightly painting these with edible gold and silver paint for added variation in colour.

4b / Alternatively, make the royal icing trees. Make a thick but pipeable Royal Icing (see page 76) and add dark green food dye. Transfer to a small piping bag and snip a medium tip. Arrange cocktail sticks [toothpicks], slightly spaced out, on baking paper. Starting a third of the way up a cocktail stick, pipe a zigzag, gradually working your way up to the tip of the cocktail stick and getting narrower as you go along, then finishing at a point. Leave to form a skin (about 1 hour), then repeat piping a zigzag

STEP 1b ▼

STEP 4a ▼

- CAKES & FROSTING -

on top. Pipe 3 or 4 trees without the cocktail stick (these are for the bottom tier). Add sprinkles to the body of some of the trees, then top some with star or snowflake-shaped sprinkles. Leave to dry hard overnight before painting with silver or gold edible paint, if liked, and peeling the trees off the paper.

4c / If you don't have time to wait overnight, you can make the trees using dark green compound chocolate. Melt the compound chocolate in 15–30-second bursts in the microwave, stirring well after each burst. When melted, transfer to a piping bag and snip a medium tip. The process is exactly the same as in step 4b, except these will set much quicker and can be used straightaway.

5 / Roll tiny red balls of sugarpaste between your palms to make 'berries'.

6 / Arrange the houses and trees around the edges of the cake. Also arrange different-shaped buildings and trees on the top of the cake. Add the red 'berries'. Transfer some leftover white buttercream to a piping bag, and use to pipe dots on the side of the cake to resemble snow falling. Use icing sugar to create the path on top of the cake. Finish with a dusting of icing sugar.

You can add little touches to this cake to make it your own! Try making tiny snowmen out of white fondant or some Christmas elves, or even Santa sneaking around!

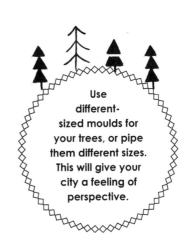

Use different-sized moulds for your trees, or pipe them different sizes. This will give your city a feeling of perspective.

- CAKES & FROSTING -

Space Turtle Cake

Turtles in space on a cake! Out of this world! What more do you need? Use any American or Italian meringue buttercream-based recipe for this. Just avoid using dark chocolate ganache and cream cheese frosting, as they are harder to work with in this way. As usual, all the design elements can be made vegan.

SERVES: 20–24

COOKIE MOON
choose a cookie recipe
   (see pages 74–75)
½ quantity of Royal Icing
   (see page 76)

SPACE TURTLES
dark blue and green
   sugarpaste

CHOCOLATE PLANETS
edible lustre dusts
a small amount of vodka
   or alcohol-based extract
500g [18oz] good-quality
   dark or white chocolate
   (no vegetable oils), finely
   chopped
OR

compound chocolate (in
   desired planet colour
   – you can use more
   traditional colours, such
   as dark blue, silver and
   gold for a galaxy effect,
   or you can use brighter
   pastel colours for a more
   abstract and dream-like
   galaxy effect, if liked

PLUS
a cake from pages 12–31,
   baked and cooled
a filling from page 60/64–5
white, pink, dark blue and
   dark purple food dyes
edible glitter (optional)
half-sphere chocolate
   moulds of different sizes
   for the planets (optional)
edible white paint

1 / Divide the buttercream (leftover from covering a cake, or make more, see pages 60 or 64–5, if required) among 4 bowls coloured as follows: white, pink, dark blue and dark purple.

2 / Working on the blank canvas (your crumb-coated cake), use an offset palette knife to smooth on different colours in different areas. You want the cake to be predominantly dark blue and dark purple, but with some streaks of white, pink and lighter blue and purple, using white to lighten. Smooth the top edge (see page 70). Place the cake in the fridge to chill.

3 / Meanwhile, make your chosen cookie recipe and cut out a large moon shape to bake (see pages 74–75). When the cookies have cooled, make the royal icing (see page 76), then outline the whole shape and flood (see page 78). Leave the royal icing to set over 4 hours.

You will have leftover cookies, but these can be enjoyed another time, or used to decorate another project.

4 / Next, shape the sugarpaste turtles (see picture on page 44) and sprinkle with edible glitter, if you like.

5 / Next, make the chocolate planets. Mix your chosen lustre dust colours with a tiny bit of vodka to make a paste. Apply the colours inside the half-squere moulds using a paintbrush (see picture on page 45) and/or flick to create a speckled effect. Leave to dry while you temper the chocolate (see page 66) or melt the compound chocolate (see note on page 44).

6 / Spoon the chocolate into your half-sphere moulds. Use a teaspoon or paintbrush to smooth the chocolate and cover the sides to leave the moulds hollow (see picture on page 45). Place all the moulds in the freezer for 10 minutes before unmoulding. If the chocolate has had long enough in the freezer and is properly tempered, it should visibly come away from the plastic and be easy to unmould.

7 / To stick the half-spheres together, warm up a plate in the microwave for 60 seconds. Place 2 half-spheres, rim-side down, on the plate for a

few seconds, then lift away. The rim will have melted away slightly, and you will be able to stick the 2 half-spheres together. Hold for a few seconds to make sure they are adhered. Leave some as half-spheres, as this will help create varying depths when decorating the cake.

Make sure your moulds are very clean, as chocolate can cling to unclean areas and cause difficulties when unmoulding.

8 / Remove the cake from the fridge. Dip a paintbrush into edible white paint and flick the paintbrush to create white specks on the cake, making it look more like a galaxy. Place the cookie moon on top of the cake. Arrange the planets on the right-hand side of the cake, pushing them into the sides of the cake. Arrange the turtles on top of the cake beside the cookie moon.

Note: If using compound chocolate, melt in the microwave using short 15–30-second bursts, stirring well after each burst. Use in the same way as the tempered chocolate.

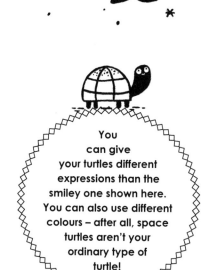

You can give your turtles different expressions than the smiley one shown here. You can also use different colours – after all, space turtles aren't your ordinary type of turtle!

STEP 4 ▼

STEP 5 ▼

STEP 6 ▼

Woodland Cake

Any of the cake recipes will complement this design. I particularly recommend this design for the Vegan Chocolate Cake (see page 15) because the chocolate and hazelnut flavours make you think about woodlands. You can also use any leftover hazelnut praline crumble for decoration and give it that *earthy* feel!

SERVES: 20–24

CHOCOLATE BARK
100g [3½oz] dark brown compound chocolate
500g [18oz] good-quality white chocolate (no vegetable oils), finely chopped, plus white oil/cocoa butter-based food colouring
OR
500g [18oz] vegan white chocolate, plus white oil/cocoa butter-based food colouring, or Homemade Vegan White Chocolate (see page 67)
OR
500g [18oz] white compound chocolate (quicker and easier, looks just as good but isn't as tasty)
*There's a large quantity of chocolate because it is easier to temper in larger quantities – leftovers can always be remelted

COOKIE DEER & CAT
choose a cookie recipe (see pages 74–75)
½ quantity of Royal Icing (see page 76)
food dyes

MERINGUE MUSHROOMS
see page 150

SUGARED BERRIES
1 medium egg white (or simple syrup if making vegan – 5 Tbsp water and 6 Tbsp caster or granulated sugar)
blueberries, blackberries and/or raspberries
granulated sugar, for coating

PLUS
a filling from pages 60–65
a cake from pages 12–31, baked and cooled
1 small handful of walnuts, hazelnuts or hazelnut praline crumbs (if using the vegan chocolate cake base)

Try making the 'bark' with dark chocolate for a different effect!

1 / Lay out a rectangular piece of smooth baking paper, about 24 x 70cm [9½ x 27½in]. Melt the dark brown compound chocolate in the microwave using 15–30-seconds bursts, stirring well after each burst. When melted, use a paintbrush to paint dots and stripes to mimic the patterns on a birch tree (see picture on page 48). Set aside.

2 / Next, if you are using white chocolate rather than compound chocolate, it will need to be tempered (see page 66) and then white oil or cocoa butter-based food colouring mixed in. Alternatively, you can skip all that tempering, and use compound chocolate. Once melted, as in Step 1, they can be used like tempered chocolate and will set firm, with a snap. They don't taste as good as real chocolate, but they are good in a rush or when the aptly named 'tempering' of chocolate tests your own temper (and this happens frequently)!

3 / Now that you have your tempered melted white chocolate or melted compound chocolate, pour this onto the prepared sheet of baking paper. Use an offset palette knife to smooth the surface on top of the painted details added earlier. Once the chocolate has set, crack the chocolate into the pieces of 'bark' that will surround the cake (see picture opposite). Arrange the chocolate bark all

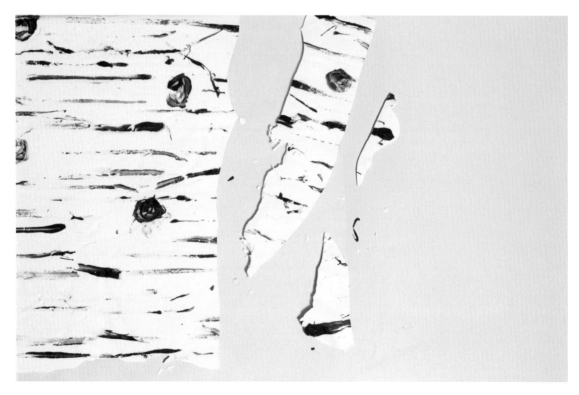

"Don't always focus on how mushroom you have for improvement – remind yourself of the things you are already good at!"

around the cake, slightly overlapping them. You may need to apply another thin layer of ganache to give the 'bark' a surface that it can stick to. The chocolate won't crack evenly, and you might end up with some smaller slivers and awkwardly shaped pieces, but this is a woodland cake and nature itself is imperfect.

4 / Select a cookie recipe from pages 74–75 and choose an animal or animals to feature on your woodland cake. I chose a deer and a cat, but you can choose whatever you want. Maybe you can create cookie fairies instead? Or an imaginary animal of your own? Maybe you can have a fondant bird sitting in a meringue bird's nest, surrounded by chocolate eggs? Or maybe you can make a little cookie version of someone you know who loves the outdoors, just enjoying the outdoors with a book? Decorate your cookies using the techniques on pages 78–81.

5 / Follow the recipe on page 150 to make different-sized meringue mushrooms.

6 / While the meringues bake, make the sugared berries. Whisk the egg white until it is less stringy, then brush onto the fruit, letting any excess drip off, and roll in granulated sugar. Set aside to dry on baking paper until no longer sticky. If making this vegan, make a simple syrup by adding the water and sugar to a small pan, then bring to a simmer over a medium heat until all the sugar has dissolved. Leave to simmer for a few more minutes, or until it seems slightly thickened. Leave to cool before brushing onto the fruit in the same way as you would with the egg white, then roll in granulated sugar.

7 / And then the fun bit! Decorate the cake with the cookie animals, meringue mushrooms, sugared berries and roughly chopped nuts (or praline crumbs – if you have them).

Easter Cake

Use any cake recipe for this cake, though of course carrot cake would make the most sense for Easter in terms of flavour. The Orange & Amaretto Rainbow Cake (see page 26) would also be a winner. I would recommend a simple white frosting that can be dyed as opposed to ganache, but you can make it your own!

This is your classic cute Easter cake full of pastel colours, Easter bunnies, carrots and Easter eggs! There's lots of scope for twists on this theme. Maybe you can have Easter ducks or chicks instead of bunnies? Or, if you struggle with royal icing piping, then make a meringue nest full of chocolate eggs for the top of the cake.

As usual, all the decorations can be made vegan; just make sure you find vegan food dyes and some vegan chocolate eggs to decorate with.

SERVES: 24–30

SUGARPASTE CARROTS
orange sugarpaste
green sugarpaste

BUNNY & EGG COOKIES, & ROYAL ICING BUNNY TOPPER
choose a cookie recipe (see pages 74–75)
1 quantity of Royal Icing (see page 76)
food dyes

WHITE GANACHE DRIP
see page 61
white gel food dye

PLUS
a cake from pages 12–31, made with 2 layers in one size and 2 layers in a different size, baked and cooled
a filling from pages 60–65

pink and green gel food dyes
200g [7oz] mini chocolate Easter eggs

1 / Apply your second coat of frosting onto the cake layers (see page 70). You can keep this plain, or if using buttercream, then play about with colours. Pastels are always a winner for Easter! To do this, divide most of the buttercream between 2 bowls and tint with different colours. A little gel dye goes a long way when you want pastel colours! Apply blobs using a palette knife, then use your cake scraper to blend together. Save 4 Tbsp white buttercream and 2 Tbsp pale pink buttercream to pipe two-tone roses later. Dye 2 Tbsp buttercream leaf-green and set the remaining white buttercream aside.

2 / Chill the cakes in the fridge while you make the various decorations.

3 / Make the sugarpaste carrots by rolling small pieces of orange sugarpaste into sausage shapes and then tapering one end into a carrot shape. Mark lines across them with a blunt knife. Make carrot tops with the green sugarpaste.

4 / Follow your chosen cookie recipe from pages 74–75, then make 3 bunnies and 3 eggs. Decorate using the techniques on pages 78–81.

5 / Use the leftover royal icing to decorate the top of the smaller cake. The cake should be chilled by now, which will help. Mark the design out using a cocktail stick [toothpick], pipe the bunny outlines and then flood (see page 78). Add the small details (pink part

STEP 5 ▼

STEP 6 ▼

This design is for a two-tiered cake, but you can easily make this one tier with fewer decorations.

of ears and facial details) after the first layer has semi-set, about 30 minutes (see picture opposite). When set, add a sugarpaste carrot for the bunny to hold.

6 / Remove the larger cake from the fridge. Prepare the ganache drip and use this to create drips on this cake (see picture opposite and page 61). You don't need to cover the top of the cake.

7 / Leave the ganache drip to set before stacking the smaller cake tier on top of the larger cake. Use the same two-tone buttercream from earlier (see Step 1, page 50) to pipe around the cake, to disguise the join between the top and base cake.

8 / Next, prepare a piping bag for the two-tone buttercream roses. Insert a 2D or 1M piping nozzle [tip] into the bag and snip an opening. Add the reserved 2 Tbsp pale pink buttercream to the bag, then close the bag and press it to ensure the buttercream touches all the sides. Open the bag again so that there is pink buttercream on the walls of the bag, but the centre is empty. Spoon in the

reserved white buttercream into the centre. Twist the top or use something to secure it, then squeeze to pipe swirls that resemble roses on top of the cake.

Tip: Tidy up the ends of your buttercream roses using a wet finger.

9 / To pipe the leaves, insert a leaf piping nozzle into a piping bag (I use a #352 tip) and snip an opening. If you don't have a leaf tip, cut an upside-down 'V' shape into the tip of the piping bag instead. Fill the piping bag with the reserved leaf-green buttercream. Pipe leaves around the roses, as this will help them look more real. Squeeze the bag, then slowly pull away while squeezing gently to create the pointy leaf tip. Try to pipe the leaves starting from the base of the buttercream roses, and angle the piping tip at 45 degrees from the cake.

10 / Place one bunny cookie on top of the top tier. Arrange the other bunnies and carrots around the cake and place the chocolate eggs all around.

Cat Paradise Cake

Cats, clouds and rainbows – it's fur-real and a dream come true! Not only will you want to live in this cake, you will also feel conflicted about wanting to eat it. Use any cake recipe with this design, though it is best to avoid dark chocolate ganache. Cream cheese frosting is fine, but it will be more difficult to create a smooth watercolour backdrop. This cake is PURRFECT for the Orange & Amaretto Rainbow Cake (see page 26), as there will be rainbows inside AND out!

SERVES: 20–24

SUGARPASTE RAINBOW
pink, yellow, red, blue and
  purple sugarpaste
edible glue

MERINGUE CLOUDS
see pages 150 and 152

SUGARPASTE CATS
white sugarpaste
edible lustre dusts or food
  dye

a small amount of vodka
  or alcohol-based extract

CHOCOLATE LADDER
100g [3½oz] brown
  compound chocolate

PLUS
a filling from pages 60–65
a cake from pages 12–31,
  baked and cooled
pale blue food dye

1 / First, make the rainbow, as this will need to set over at least 2 nights (you can speed this up by placing it in a warm [but switched off!] oven). Roll out long tubes of each colour, then mould around a round cookie cutter. Brush on a little edible glue to adhere the different colours together. Trim the excess so that the bottoms are neat and straight. Leave to set.

2 / Divide the filling (leftover from crumb-coating the cake, or make more, see pages 60–65) between 2 bowls and tint one pale blue.

3 / Working on the blank canvas (your crumb-coated cake), use an offset palette knife to smooth on different colours. Use a cake scraper to create a dreamy watercolour sky-like canvas. Smooth in the top edge (see page 70). Chill the cake in the fridge.

4 / Meanwhile, make at least 4 meringue clouds of different sizes (see pages 150 and 152).

5 / Shape the 2 cats from white sugarpaste, then paint details using edible lustre dust or food dye mixed with a little vodka.

6 / Place the compound chocolate in a bowl and melt in the microwave in 15–30-second bursts, stirring well after each burst. Transfer to a piping bag and prepare a sheet of baking paper. Pipe 2 parallel lines onto the baking paper, each about 5cm [2in] apart and about the same length as the height of the cake. Pipe horizontal lines between the 2 parallel lines to make a ladder and leave to set.

7 / Place the rainbow on top of the cake, tilting it slightly into the cake so that it is secured. Stick meringue clouds up the side of the cake and on top. Peel the ladder off the baking paper, then lean against the cake. Place a cat at the base of the ladder looking upwards, then the second cat at the top of the ladder looking downwards.

Whale Underwater Cake

This design works perfectly with any cake recipe that has a buttercream frosting. Avoid cream cheese, as it will be difficult to create the whale design.

This is a single-tiered cake, but you can scale it up and create a very grand cake that reflects the depths of the ocean. Try to add a bottom tier with a blue ganache drip effect (see page 61). You can also create sea creatures out of sugarpaste to create a whole underwater world. There are a lot of elements to this cake, but you can just keep it simple and omit some of them if you prefer. The image of the whale along with the colourful coral is so striking and effective that it doesn't need much more, but all the extras are extremely fun to make and decorate with!

As usual, all the design elements can be made vegan.

SERVES: 20–24

MERINGUE SEA FOAM
Meringue recipe (see page 150)

SEAWEED BUBBLE SHARDS
liquid glucose
orange, green, blue and yellow food dyes

ISOMALT CORAL
ready-tempered isomalt (see note on page 59) in any colours you wish

CORAL TUILES
1 Tbsp sunflower oil
30g [3⅔ Tbsp] plain [all-purpose] flour
270ml [1¼ cups] water

green and orange food dyes

PLUS
a filling from pages 60–65
a cake from pages 12–31, baked and cooled
pale blue, dark blue and white food dyes
edible white paint

1 / First, cover your crumb-coated cake with a second coat of pale blue buttercream or filling. Return the cake to the fridge or freezer to chill.

2 / Make the meringue (see page 150), then crumble into pieces when baked and cooled.

3 / Next, prepare the seaweed bubbles. Preheat the oven to 150°C [300°F/Gas mark 2]. This is so surprisingly simple and effective to do. Squeeze a few blobs of liquid glucose onto a baking sheet lined with baking paper or a silicone mat. Add a small dot of food dye to the centre of each (see page 58). Place in the oven for 1 hour (avoid opening the oven door during this time, as this might cause the bubbles to pop). Or you can add a dot of food dye to either end, and they will merge and blend together naturally in the oven. Play about with different sizes and shapes of glucose. That's IT! The sugar will caramelize, the colour will spread and the sugar will start forming a bubbly pattern all on its own. You can create a lot of random and interesting shapes and colour combinations, and all will be beautiful.

4 / Meanwhile, make the isomalt coral. Fill a large deep bowl with lots of ice cubes. Melt the isomalt in a heatproof bowl in the microwave (follow the instructions on the packet) until liquid, then pour the isomalt over the ice cubes. Wait a few minutes, then pull out the isomalt, which will have now set. Some ice cubes will be attached – you can gently pry some of these away, but leave the ones that are trapped to melt in their own time. Repeat to make more coral and in different colours! You can play about with how much isomalt you pour in and its viscosity/temperature and how this affects the finished result.

The isomalt looks so impressive but it's extremely simple. It's like magic seeing the different shapes the isomalt forms as it sets over the ice cubes. Just be careful because isomalt is very hot when it is liquid.

5 / Next, make the coral tuiles. Heat the sunflower oil in a small saucepan. In a small bowl, whisk the flour and water together, then divide between 2 bowls and colour one green and the other orange. Add a ladleful of the batter into the saucepan and immediately step right back, as the oil and water spits A LOT. When the spitting subsides and the scene is calmer (within a minute or two), use a spatula to

carefully remove the tuile from the oil and place it on paper towels to drain. Repeat to make a few seaweed tuiles of different colours.

This is quite the fancy chef technique and is used to decorate beautifully plated desserts. It is simple to make, but it's messy. And believe me when I say you will need to step back, and the pan will be hissing very loudly when you put the batter in.

6 / Next, create a whale template by tracing a whale design onto a rectangular piece of paper or card, and cut out. You can find whale templates online.

7 / Divide the buttercream between 2 bowls and colour 1 bowl dark blue. Leave the other bowl white. Remove the chilled cake from the fridge or freezer and press the template against the side of the cake where you want the whale design to go. Use a cocktail stick [toothpick] to indent the buttercream around the template. Remove the template, then use a palette knife to spread the dark blue and white buttercream within the lines of the whale shape (see picture opposite).

STEP 3 ▼

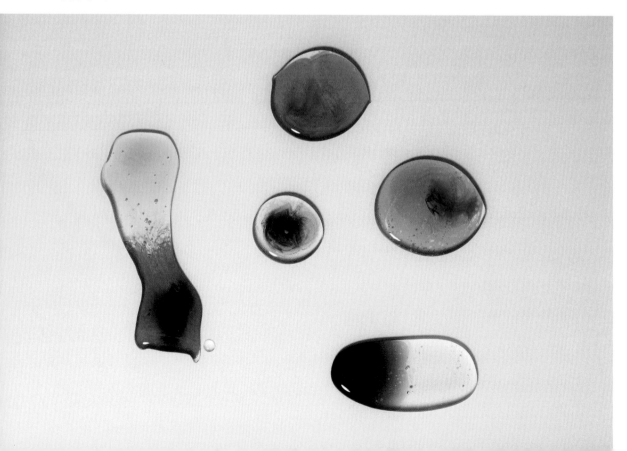

8 / Dip a paintbrush in edible white paint, and use this to flick onto the whale – this helps to suggest more movement with splashes here and there.

9 / Finish by arranging all the different elements you made earlier. Place a few larger pieces of isomalt coral on top, along with some liquid glucose shards and coral tuiles. Sprinkle some crushed meringue underneath. Arrange isomalt coral, coral tuiles and bubble seaweed on one side of the base of the cake. Add more crushed meringue at the base of the cake.

Note: Isomalt is a sugar substitute that does not crystallize or change colour when heated, therefore its colour remains clear and vibrant, and is perfect for cake decorating techniques such as this. If you buy pre-coloured and ready-tempered isomalt, you can melt it repeatedly and it won't change colour or consistency. It can be quite expensive, but it's just fun to see what shapes it will form when poured onto the ice cubes. If you can't find this ingredient, you can easily leave it out and the cake will still look lovely!

You can use any colours you want for the whale – it doesn't have to be realistic. You can make a unicorn whale with pinks and lilacs instead, or a more earthy blue and green whale. You can also pair these colours with the corals and seaweeds.

Try creating designs for other underwater creatures, such as an octopus, shark, fish, sea turtle, etc... there's lots of options!

American Buttercream

This makes a large quantity. It should be enough to fill and crumb-coat all of the tiered cake recipes. There should also be leftovers for the second buttercream coat. Halve this quantity if you are not covering the top and sides of the cake. You can make three-quarters of this recipe if you are just crumb-coating your cake. This buttercream is quick and easy to make, which is helpful when you're in a rush! You can flavour it in so many different ways – vanilla, rosewater, orange or lemon zest, raspberry powder, coffee, almond, etc. It helps to have a stand mixer due to the quantities, but you can still make it with a handheld electric whisk.

MAKES: ENOUGH TO FILL, CRUMB-COAT AND COVER A TIERED CAKE

550g [2½ cups] unsalted butter, at room temperature

800g [5¾ cups] icing [confectioners'] sugar

milk, to thin

Place the butter and icing sugar in a stand mixer (or use a handheld electric whisk) fitted with a balloon whisk attachment and beat until light and fluffy. Add milk, 1 Tbsp at a time, to achieve a spreadable consistency. Now add any flavourings.

That's it! Use on your cake right now, or cover with plastic wrap if not (as it will form a crust). Refrigerate if not using for a few days; it should be fine for 2–3 days at room temperature.

Cream Cheese Frosting

This has a slight tang from the cream cheese, which works well with cakes that have warming spices such as cinnamon and ginger. It remains firm, so can be piped and used to cover cakes. Just be careful not to overmix it!

MAKES: ENOUGH TO FILL, CRUMB-COAT AND COVER A TIERED CAKE

115g [½ cup] salted butter, at room temperature, chopped

600g [4¼ cups] icing [confectioners'] sugar

300g [1¼ cups] whole cream cheese

Place the butter in a stand mixer (or use a handheld electric whisk) fitted with a balloon whisk attachment and beat until smooth and softened. Add half the icing sugar and beat until combined. Add the cream cheese and the rest of the sugar and whisk until combined. Don't overmix, or the frosting will become too soft.

Coloured Ganache Controlled Drips

Controlled drips running down a cake can make it really pop! Make sure the cake is well chilled beforehand and that your ganache is a good dripping consistency – if it is too warm it will be too thin and run too fast, but if it is too cold it will be too thick and blobby rather than elegant. Check for the correct consistency by practising some drips down a mug with a metal spoon (see picture on page 52). If your ganache is too warm, chill it for a minute (keep a close eye on it). If it is too cool, microwave it for 5–10 seconds. When you are ready, use your spoon (or a piping bag) to gently push a few drips down the side of the cake. Drips look best when the spaces between them are equal, but they can vary in length.

MAKES: SEVERAL DRIPS!

WHITE OR COLOURED DRIP
60ml [¼ cup] double [heavy] cream
130g [4½oz] white chocolate, roughly chopped into small pieces

VEGAN WHITE OR COLOURED DRIP
60ml [¼ cup] coconut milk
130g [4½oz] vegan white chocolate, roughly chopped into small pieces

PLUS
gel food colour (normally this would cause chocolate to seize, but in this case it is fine because cream/coconut milk already contain a lot of water)

1a / For the regular ganache drip, pour the cream into a small pan and heat over a medium heat until it just starts to bubble (or heat in the microwave for about 45 seconds).

2a / Add the white chocolate pieces, making sure they are fully submerged and covered and leave the mixture to stand for 2 minutes (set a timer).

3a / Stir until all the chocolate has melted.

4a / Add gel food dye and stir in. Leave the mixture to cool until it is the correct consistency.

You will find that the ganache drip is a pale yellow colour rather than pure white, so if you want it white you will need to add some white food dye. If you want gold or silver drips, use the ganache drip as it is, but paint the drips with edible silver or gold food paint after they have set. Also try using drips of different colours on one cake!

1b / If you don't have vegan white chocolate and are looking for a vegan ganache drip, pour the coconut milk into a small pan and heat over a medium heat until it just starts to bubble (or heat in the microwave for about 45 seconds).

2b / Add the vegan white chocolate pieces, making sure they are fully submerged and covered and leave the mixture to stand for 2 minutes (set a timer).

3b / Stir until all the chocolate has melted.

4b / Add gel food dye and stir in. Leave the mixture to cool until it is the correct consistency.

Alternatively, vegan royal icing (see page 76) works for a ganache drip, too!

Orange Curd for Cakes

This makes a delicious curd that's suitable for filling cakes. It makes a larger quantity than the recipe designed for filling macarons on page 126, and it results in a different consistency. Use it in the Blueberry Cake with Orange Curd on page 24 and allow to drip temptingly down the sides of the cake, or spoon it neatly in the centre of a buttercream dam (see pages 68–69).

MAKES: ENOUGH TO USE AS PARTIAL FILLING FOR A LARGE CAKE

2 large eggs, plus 2 large
    egg yolks
grated zest and juice of
    2 large oranges
180g [1 scant cup] caster
    or granulated sugar
120g [½ cup] unsalted
    butter

1 / Place the eggs, egg yolks, orange juice and zest, sugar and butter in a heatproof bowl and stir with a balloon whisk until combined.

2 / Place the heatproof bowl on top of a pan of hot water on the stove, making sure the bottom of the bowl isn't touching the water, and whisk constantly for 10–15 minutes until the mixture has thickened (you will notice the foam start to disappear) and coats the back of a spoon.

3 / Pour the curd into a bowl, cover with plastic wrap (touching the surface to avoid a skin forming) and chill in the fridge for 45 minutes or in the freezer for 15–20 minutes until cool. You can strain the curd before transferring to a bowl if you have any cooked egg, or if you prefer not to have the zest. I like to keep the zest in, as it adds great flavour and it seems wasteful to discard it!

Italian Meringue Buttercream

This recipe makes a large quantity. It should be enough to fill and crumb-coat all of the tiered cake recipes. There should also be leftovers for the second buttercream coat. Halve this quantity if you are not covering the top and sides of the cake. You can make three-quarters of this recipe if you are just crumb-coating your cake. It helps to have a stand mixer for this recipe, as you will need to be whisking the egg whites and adding sugar while also keeping an eye on the temperature of the sugar syrup.

This buttercream is silky smooth, and less sweet than the American-style buttercream on page 60. It is so easy to work with and sets very firm in the fridge, so when you slice the cake, the layers of buttercream will be very distinct. This is my preferred buttercream for tiered cakes – it just takes a little more time to make but is so worth it.

This is unflavoured, but as with the American buttercream, you can flavour it in so many different ways. Try vanilla, rosewater, orange or lemon zest, raspberry powder, coffee, almond, etc.

MAKES: ENOUGH TO FILL, CRUMB-COAT AND COVER A TIERED CAKE

225g [8oz] egg whites (from about 7–8 medium eggs)
560g [2¾ cups] caster or granulated sugar

225ml [1 cup] water
½ tsp cream of tartar
675g [3 cups] unsalted butter, at room temperature

1 / Place the egg whites in a stand mixer (or use a handheld electric whisk) fitted with the balloon whisk attachment. Add half the sugar to a separate bowl.

2 / Put the remaining sugar and the water into a pan and heat over a medium-high heat, stirring occasionally to dissolve all the sugar. Once the mixture starts bubbling, don't stir.

3 / As soon as the syrup starts bubbling, start whisking the egg whites in the stand mixer. Add the cream of tartar once it is frothy, then when it reaches soft peaks, start gradually adding the sugar, 1 Tbsp at a time, until thick and shiny. You will need to time this with the sugar syrup reaching 115°C [239°F]. If necessary, you can slow down the mixer (but don't stop it) or reduce the heat for the sugar syrup. When all the sugar has been added to the meringue and the sugar syrup has reached 115°C [239°F], pour the syrup in a thin stream down the side of the mixer, while mixing on maximum speed. Be careful not to slow the speed of the mixer, or to pour the syrup directly onto the whisk, as it may splash and it is very hot. Leave to whisk on high speed (this helps to cool

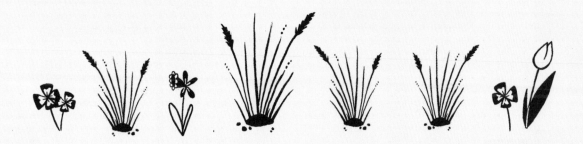

the meringue faster) for 20–30 minutes, or until the bottom of the bowl feels like it is at room temperature – this sounds like a long time, but there is so much sugar in the meringue that you won't overbeat it. At this point you can add the butter.

4 / Add 3–4 cubes of the butter at a time, beating well after each addition. Continue until all the butter has been added. The mixture will go from firm to becoming more liquid, and this is completely normal – just keep adding more butter. When you have added all the butter, the mixture will return to being fluffy and the perfect consistency to spread on your cake. At this point you can add flavourings. Use right away, or cover with plastic wrap if using later in the day.

5 / You can refrigerate this buttercream for up to a week, but you will need to follow a few steps to reconstitute it. When you remove it from the fridge, it will be very hard like a block of butter, so you will need to soften it by heating it in the microwave in 15-second bursts. You will need to be patient and make sure that the butter does not melt. If the butter does melt, pop it back in the fridge to firm. When you have brought the buttercream to room temperature, it still won't look right, but that's fine. Transfer the buttercream to a stand mixer (or use a handheld electric whisk) and whisk on high speed until smooth and creamy again. Be patient; if it is not coming together, it either needs whisking longer or bringing to the correct temperature.

- CAKES & FROSTING -

Tempering Chocolate

If chocolate is melted and not correctly tempered, then it will take a long time to set, and it will be sticky and flexible rather than snap. It won't taste as nice, and it will be more difficult to position around the cake. So, first you will need to set up a bain-marie – you will need a heatproof bowl (which is clean and completely dry) to sit over a pan of boiling water (making sure the bottom of the bowl does not touch the boiling water). Put three-quarters of the finely chopped chocolate in the heatproof bowl, and set aside a quarter of the chocolate for 'seeding' the chocolate later. Stir the chocolate until it has melted and its temperature is 43°C [109°F] for white chocolate or 46°C [115°F] for dark chocolate (you will need a thermometer). Start taking the chocolate off the heat before it reaches the desired temperature, because you will find that the temperature suddenly shoots up from the bowl, getting very hot. Then add the reserved chunks of chocolate to the bowl, stirring constantly. Keep stirring until the temperature comes down to 28–29°C [82–84°F] for white chocolate or 32°C [90°F] for dark chocolate. Now your chocolate is tempered and ready to use. You can check it is tempered by leaving some to set on the back of a spoon. It should set within 5 minutes. Be careful not to let any water touch the chocolate, otherwise it will seize and become unusable.

When chocolate is properly tempered, you can pour it into moulds and it will release easily from them. The chocolate will also come out beautifully smooth and shiny. Just make sure that any moulds you use are completely clean and dry. Seeing shiny chocolate pop out of a mould is one of the best feelings!

The best way to explain tempering (without going into the science) is that once you melt chocolate, it becomes untrained and has a 'bad temper'. So it needs 'teaching' (aka tempering) to become well behaved once more! The chocolate chunks that you add in are like the 'teachers', and you need to keep stirring constantly so that all the melted chocolate gets a chance to learn from them.

The temperature needed can vary depending on the brand of chocolate and cocoa butter content. The best chocolate you can use for tempering is couverture chocolate. This isn't the cheapest, but it has a high cocoa butter content, which makes it easy to work with and comes in 'callets' or little chips, so there is no need to chop it up. Packets of couverture chocolate will specify the temperatures to use for tempering.

COMPOUND CHOCOLATE
Alternatively, you can use compound chocolate (sometimes referred to as Candy Melts/candy coating/coating chocolate). This does not contain cocoa butter, so it does not need tempering and is cheaper to buy. However, many people find that it does not taste as nice as 'real' chocolate. Compound chocolate is a good choice if you only need to work with a small amount of chocolate (tempering is easier with a larger amount of chocolate, as the temperature changes are steadier) or you are in a rush – or you just don't like tempering!

Homemade Vegan White Chocolate

MAKES: 500G [18OZ]

240g [1 cup plus 1 Tbsp] cocoa butter (set aside 50g [¼ cup] of this if tempering)

200g [1½ cups minus 1 Tbsp] icing [confectioners'] sugar

60g [¼ cup] soy milk powder (important that this is powdered and not flour)

1 vanilla pod [bean], seeds scraped out (you can use 1–2 tsp vanilla extract, but make sure it does not contain any water)

AND/OR white cocoa butter-based food colouring

1 / Melt the cocoa butter over a bain-marie (see opposite), stirring intermittently, until completely melted.

2 / Sift the icing sugar and soy milk powder together, then gradually add to the melted cocoa butter and whisk over a low heat until completely incorporated and smooth.

3 / At this point, you can add vanilla and/or cocoa butter-based food colouring, if using. Then the chocolate can be used as desired and placed in the freezer for a few minutes to set. However, this won't be tempered.

4 / If you want to temper your chocolate, bring it to 42°C [108°F], then add the solid lump of tempered cocoa butter you previously set aside. Stir constantly until the temperature comes down to 29°C [84°F]. You may need to place the bowl over ice just to cool it down a little faster. Then mould or use however you like. It should set at room temperature, but you can place it in the freezer if using moulds.

You can use this to decorate cakes, but you can also just temper it and pour it into chocolate bar moulds, to snack on yourself or give away. It has a high cocoa butter content, so it melts in your mouth, but the soy milk powder gives it body so that it is not too intensely rich. I find that the white chocolate from supermarkets tastes mostly of sugar, which is not what you want, whereas this is sweet but not overpoweringly, so you still get the lovely cocoa butter flavour coming through. Because commercial chocolate makers have specialist machines to get their chocolate completely smooth, this homemade version can taste a little on the grainy side. If that bothers you, you can grind the soy milk powder a little finer in a food processor or spice grinder.

Cake Decorating Tips & Ideas

LEVELLING

Sometimes your baked cake might dome upwards in the middle, which is not ideal for stacking. Level your cakes by using a serrated knife and judging by eye, or use a purpose-made cake leveller. This means you can reward yourself with the cake cut-offs...

ASSEMBLING CAKE LAYERS

First, you want to use a cake board that is just slightly larger than your cakes. Put a blob of frosting on the cake board, then place the first cake layer on top. The buttercream will stop it sliding about! Cover the cake with a solid layer of room-temperature buttercream (thickness comes down to personal preference, but you don't want 2.5-cm [1-in] thick frosting!). You can pipe this buttercream on, or just spread it on with an offset spatula. If using jam and/or curd, see the 'dam' technique below. Place the second cake on top. If you're planning on covering the sides of the cake, it can be helpful if the buttercream squeezes out of the side of the cake a little bit, then repeat until the last cake layer is placed on top.

STACKING MULTIPLE TIERS

When stacking a cake with different sizes of tier (like the Easter Cake on page 51), ensure that each tier has a cake board underneath; use thinner cake boards for the tiers higher up. Also make sure each tier is properly chilled before stacking. For 3 or more tiers or softer, fragile cakes, it helps to use dowels. Thick straws work well, too. You need to insert one down the centre, and then a few around it. Trim them so that they stick out a tiny bit above the cake and are all the same height. The aim of the dowels is that they – rather than the actual cake – take the weight of the tiers above.

DAM

This is useful when you are working with softer fillings in between cake layers, such as jam or curd. You pipe a 'dam' of buttercream (see picture opposite) around the circumference of the cake so that it can be filled with the softer filling, which then won't ooze out.

CRUMB COATING

This is the first coat of buttercream you apply all over your cake in order to stop the pesky crumbs sneaking into your second layer, and so that you can play about with colour on your second layer. Chill your crumb-coated cake in the fridge or freezer before applying the finishing coat.

To crumb-coat your cake layers, smooth buttercream all over the tops and sides of the cake using an offset spatula. Then, to get this as smooth as possible, it helps to use a turntable and cake scraper. Hold the scraper at a 45-degree angle and slowly spin the turntable to get a smooth finish. You may have to do this a couple of times.

If you are working on a cake that doesn't have too many crumbs when you coat it, then it is sometimes effective to leave it as a 'semi-naked' cake, which has some of the cake peaking out through the buttercream and can look very elegant (see picture above). To get an even finish on this, warm the cake scraper that you are using by running it under hot water – the heat helps make everything nice and smooth.

To smooth the top, use an offset spatula to smooth the rough edges inwards. Again, use a warm offset spatula to get an even finish on this. Sometimes it can look effective to leave the top edges rough and uneven (see page 39), especially if this contrasts with a neat and smooth design elsewhere.

FINISHING THE BUTTERCREAM COAT IN DIFFERENT WAYS
This is the best part because you can play around with COLOUR! The crumb coat should now be properly chilled and firm, so you can apply colour and texture without disturbing it. Think of it as a blank canvas, and the second coat as art.

If you add a few different blobs of colour and smooth with your cake scraper, you can achieve a beautiful watercolour effect (see picture opposite, above).

Alternatively, you can play with texture: apply different colours using an offset spatula. Smooth some bits, and allow the texture to show through on others.

You can also paint with buttercream using a palette knife almost like an oil painting. This can create some beautiful effects (see picture opposite, below).

Semolina Shortbread

This dough can be rolled out thinly and used to cut out shapes, though you will need to take care, as it has a high fat-to-flour ratio and is a little more delicate. If you are new to working with cookie dough, use this only for simpler shapes.

MAKES: 24–30

200g [¾ cup plus 2 Tbsp] salted butter
85g [7 Tbsp] caster or granulated sugar

200g [1½ cups] plain [all-purpose] flour
70g [¼ cup plus 2 Tbsp] fine semolina

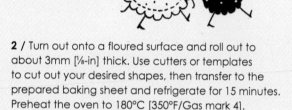

1 / Line a baking sheet with baking paper. Beat the butter and sugar until smooth and fluffy. Add the flour and semolina and mix until just combined. The dough should be slightly sticky, but soft and easy to handle. If needed, wrap in plastic wrap and chill in the fridge for 10–15 minutes until firm enough to roll out.

2 / Turn out onto a floured surface and roll out to about 3mm [⅛-in] thick. Use cutters or templates to cut out your desired shapes, then transfer to the prepared baking sheet and refrigerate for 15 minutes. Preheat the oven to 180°C [350°F/Gas mark 4].

3 / Bake for 10–15 minutes until just lightly browned at the edges. Leave to cool for 10 minutes on the sheet, then gently transfer to a rack to finish cooling.

Ginger Cookies

These ginger cookies hold their shape when baking, which makes them a perfect go-to recipe for decorated, shaped treats. Not to mention that lovely cinnamon, ginger and clove flavour – it makes your whole house smell like Christmas!

MAKES: 18–24

150g [⅔ cup] salted butter
120g [½ cup plus 1½ Tbsp] dark muscovado [soft brown] sugar

2 tsp black treacle [molasses]
2 Tbsp beaten egg
2 Tbsp ground ginger

¾ Tbsp ground cinnamon
¼ tsp ground cloves
225g [1⅔ cups] plain [all-purpose] flour

1 / Line a baking sheet with baking paper. Place the butter, sugar and treacle in a stand mixer (or use a handheld electric whisk) fitted with the balloon whisk attachment and mix on high speed until fluffy. Add the beaten egg and spices and mix briefly. Add the flour and combine into a ball with your hands. Turn out onto a floured surface and roll out to the thickness of a coin. Use cutters or templates

to cut out your desired shapes, then transfer to the prepared baking sheet and refrigerate for 15 minutes. Preheat the oven to 170°C [340°F/Gas mark 3].

2 / Bake for 10–12 minutes until just beginning to colour. Leave to cool for 10 minutes on the sheet, then gently transfer to a rack to finish cooling.

Basic Vegan Shortbread

This shortbread has just a hint of sweetness and is perfect for covering with royal icing. If eating plain, sprinkle some sugar on top just before baking. You can add a little more sugar to the dough, but this will make the shortbread chewier.

MAKES: 24–30

225g [1⅔ cups] plain [all-purpose] flour
130g [⅔ cup] organic extra virgin coconut oil (solid and scoopable)

40g [3¼ Tbsp] caster or granulated sugar
30–50g [2–3½ Tbsp] cold water

1 / Line a baking sheet with baking paper. Place the flour in a bowl, add the scoopable coconut oil and, using your fingers, rub the oil into the flour. Stir in the sugar, then add just enough cold water to bring the dough together into a ball.

2 / Turn the dough out onto a floured surface and roll out to 3–5mm [⅛–¼in] thick. Use cutters or templates to cut out your desired shapes, then transfer to the prepared baking sheet and chill for 15 minutes. Preheat the oven to 180°C [350°F/Gas mark 4].

3 / Bake for 10–15 minutes until just starting to colour at the edges. Leave to cool on the baking sheet for 5 minutes, then gently transfer to a rack to finish cooling.

Vegan Ginger Cookies

This delicious cookie holds it shape when baking and has a lovely balance of warm spices to make you feel cosy and content.

MAKES: 18–24

225g [1⅔ cups] plain [all-purpose] flour
130g [⅔ cup] organic extra virgin coconut oil (solid and scoopable)

130g [⅔ cup] dark muscovado [soft brown] sugar
2 Tbsp ground ginger
¾ Tbsp ground cinnamon

¼ tsp ground cloves
2 tsp black treacle [molasses]
cold water, to combine

1 / Line a baking sheet with baking paper. Place the flour in a large bowl, add the scoopable coconut oil and rub the oil into the flour. Stir in the sugar and spices, then add the treacle and just enough cold water to bring the dough together into a ball. Turn out onto a floured surface and roll out to the thickness of a coin. Use cutters or templates to cut out your desired shapes, then transfer to the prepared baking sheet and refrigerate for 15 minutes. Preheat the oven to 170°C [340°F/Gas mark 3].

2 / Bake for 10–12 minutes until the surface is firmer. Leave to cool for 5 minutes on the baking sheet, then gently transfer to a wire rack to finish cooling.

Cookie Decorating Tips & Ideas

ROYAL ICING CONSISTENCY

Different people like to work with different consistencies, but I like to work with what is called a '15-second icing'. This means that after stirring the mixture, the surface will return back to its former smooth state in about 15 seconds. This consistency will work for both outlining AND flooding, so is much easier than making two batches. The definition of '15-second' icing varies for everyone, though, as everyone counts differently, so it's mostly about practising and getting the feel for the correct consistency. My royal icing recipe should get you to roughly the consistency you will need, so hopefully you can work from there!

If icing can get back to being smooth in 15 seconds, maybe you can, too! Take your time with this.

ROYAL ICING RECIPE
This makes enough for a decent number of cookies

40g [2⅔ Tbsp] egg white (or aquafaba [see page 30] for a vegan version)
210g [1½ cups] icing [confectioners'] sugar,

plus extra egg white (or aquafaba) and icing [confectioners'] sugar to adjust and get the right consistency

Use a stand mixer (or handheld electric whisk) fitted with a balloon whisk attachment to combine the egg white (or aquafaba) and icing sugar until you get a smooth consistency. Then add tiny amounts of extra egg white (or aquafaba) and/or icing sugar to get the right consistency. Add food dye to colour as desired! That is it!

USEFUL THINGS
cocktail sticks [toothpicks]
edible ink pen
tiny paintbrushes
edible lustre dust & vodka
 or alcohol-based extract
edible paint

DISPOSABLE PIPING BAGS

Good disposable piping bags are your friends! You want to find some that don't have a seam, as this can get in the way when piping. For outlining and for piping intricate details, snip a teeny-tiny tip from your piping bag. For flooding, snip a slightly bigger tip (depends on how big an area you are flooding). That's it. No need for piping tips, which make washing up a lot harder! If you ever snip a tip that is too big, or want to change to a smaller opening, then just pop the piping bag into another piping bag. Snip the tip as desired, and continue!

ICING PREP, PLANNING & LAYERING

It helps to draw a guide of where you will pipe the outlines directly on the cookie. It also helps to know what colours you are going to use before you start so that you can mix them all up and put into piping bags. I don't always know what colours I will want, so I always leave some white royal icing in a bowl that I can dye later. Just make sure you cover the bowl with plastic wrap, otherwise the surface will crust up quickly.

Sometimes things come to you as you go along. A vague idea is all you need – that's OK, too.

Cookie decorating does take some forward planning if you want to do more than one layer, in which case you need to wait for a few hours for the first layer to dry before working on the second, or third. For instance, you may have a background layer using the wet-on-wet technique (see page 81) to create a sunset, then after that dries you might want to pipe some mountains on top and add some painted birds. Or you might want to pipe some tiny flower detailing on a dress. The layer underneath needs to be dry before you can do all these things. While your cookies are drying, set them aside and find something else to do (or not do!) to relax.

OUTLINING

When you first start piping royal icing in a neat line, you might find it tricky. It is not like dragging a pen across a surface. You need to pipe, lift and ease the line where you need it. Don't expect to get it perfect the first time – practise and you will get better.

FLOODING

No, not the psychological therapy used to overcome phobias – this is much nicer! Once you have planned and then outlined your cookie, it is time to flood. All you are doing is filling the space inside, and the outline will stop it leaking over. Use a cocktail stick [toothpick] to even it out and get rid of any bubbles before it sets.

LACEWORK

On a plain cookie background or a completely set, flooded base, create a grid of tiny squares by piping thin lines with the finest piping tip.

Fill the grid with dots to create a pattern. You can create any pattern you like. Try using different colours, too (a bit like cross stitch!)

WET-ON-WET

This is when you use 2 different colours and a cocktail stick to create some interesting effects. This is useful for polka dots, hearts, flowers and scenes that involve a beautiful gradient of colour, such as sunsets, skies, seas and fire. Drag the cocktail stick [toothpick] (or you can use a scribe tool) through the colours, working quickly before the icing sets!

- COOKIES & ICING -

PAINTING ON ROYAL ICING

When your royal icing is completely dry (4–6 hours, but I usually wait overnight to be sure), you can paint on it using food dyes or edible lustre dusts mixed with vodka (which evaporates quicker than water). You can also brush on lustre dusts to give depth, and draw on the icing using edible ink. Anything you can paint or draw in paper you can do on an iced cookie. Fine details can also be drawn onto royal icing (only once it has completely set!) using an edible ink pen.

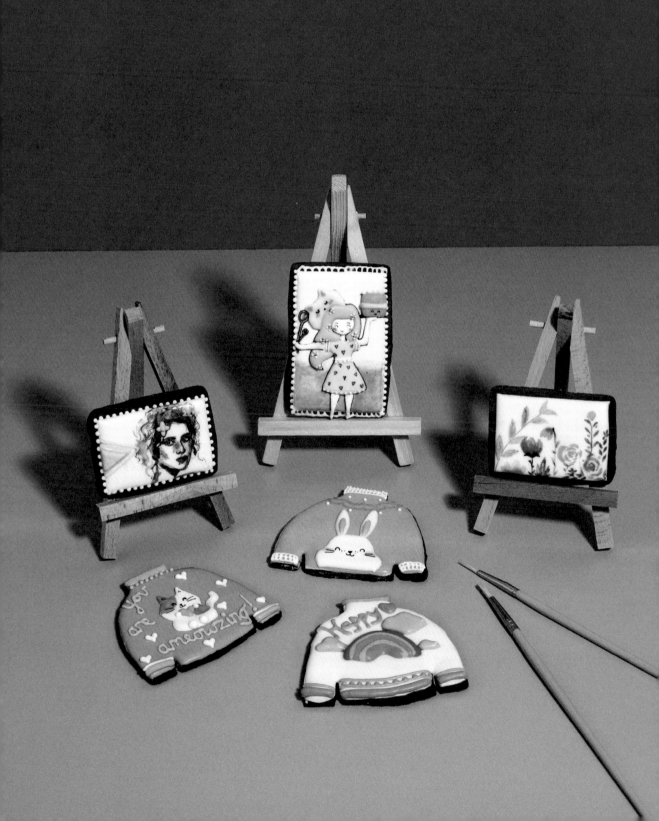

Breads

Tangzhong Cat Buns

These rolls are not just cute, they are the softest, fluffiest bread you can find, and that's thanks to the 'tangzhong' technique. This is credited as being a Japanese method, but became popular with home cooks and in Chinese bakeries after a Chinese woman called Yvonne Chen wrote a book about it. You might hear this kind of bread referred to as hokkaido milk bread, Asian milk bread or shokupan.

Tangzhong is simply about making a roux with some of the flour and water, which is then cooled and added to the dough mixture. This roux essentially locks in the liquid, and helps to give the final bread a higher moisture content. The resulting bread is soft, cloud-like and stays fresher for longer. Making the roux takes just 5 minutes of your time, but completely transforms this bread.

MAKES: 9

TANGZHONG PASTE
25g [3 Tbsp] strong white [bread] flour, plus extra for dusting
100ml [⅓ cup plus 1 Tbsp] water

DOUGH
125ml [½ cup] whole milk, plus extra for brushing
30g [2 Tbsp] unsalted butter
oil, for oiling
10g [2½ tsp] caster or granulated sugar
1 tsp salt
1 large egg
350g [2½ cups] strong white [bread] flour
7g [2¼ tsp] fast-action dried [active dry] yeast

PLUS
1 egg, lightly beaten, for brushing
brown food dye
a small amount of vodka or alcohol-based extract
black edible pen or Royal Icing (see page 76), dyed black

1 / First, make the tangzhong paste. Using a balloon whisk, mix the flour and water together in a pan until smooth. Place the pan over a low-medium heat and stir constantly with a spatula until thickened to a pudding-like consistency. If you have a thermometer the paste should reach 65°C [149°F] before you take it off the heat. Transfer the tangzhong to a small bowl, cover with plastic wrap (making sure this touches the surface of the tangzhong) and chill in the freezer for 10 minutes.

2 / Meanwhile, for the dough, warm the milk in the microwave. It should be warm but not hot. Melt the butter, too. Lightly oil a large bowl and grease a 20-cm [8-in] square baking tin, then set aside.

3 / Place the milk and butter in a large bowl and add the sugar and salt. Add the chilled tangzhong to the bowl along with the egg and whisk together.

4 / Add the flour and yeast to the mixture. If using a stand mixer, just allow the machine to knead for 10 minutes with the dough hook attachment. If working by hand, use a wooden spoon to combine everything into a shaggy ball of dough, then turn out onto a floured surface.

5 / Knead by hand for about 10–15 minutes. The dough will be sticky to start with, but avoid adding too much flour – it will gradually become less sticky as you knead it. If the dough sticks to the surface, use a dough scraper to scrape it off. Keep kneading until the dough is smooth; it will still be a little tacky, but that is normal.

6 / Place the dough in the oiled bowl and cover with plastic wrap. Leave to rise in a warm place until doubled in size. This takes about 1 hour, but it depends on the temperature of your kitchen.

7 / When the dough has doubled in size, turn it out onto a lightly floured surface and knock back. Form into 9 balls, weighing 65g [2¼oz] each. Shape them by tucking the dough under to create a smooth surface. There will be leftover dough – this is to shape the ears and paws.

8 / Shape the small balls of dough into ears and paws for the cats (see picture below). You can brush on a little milk to help them stick. Shape a tail for one of the buns – this will look like the cat has turned around. Work fast to avoid the dough forming a skin.

9 / Place the dough balls in the prepared square tin. Cover with lightly oiled plastic wrap and leave to prove in a warm place until roughly doubled in size. The time this takes varies depending on the temperature of your kitchen, but won't be as long as the first rise. You are looking for the dough to have nearly doubled in size and spring back halfway when lightly pressed with a finger.

10 / About 15 minutes before the end of the proving time, preheat the oven to 180°C [350°F/Gas mark 4].

11 / Brush the beaten egg on top of the buns just before baking. Bake for 20 minutes until lightly golden brown. You will need to cover the buns with foil after 5–10 minutes, just to prevent them browning too much.

12 / Transfer to a rack and leave to cool completely.

13 / Paint coloured patches on the cold buns using a little brown food dye mixed with a tiny bit of vodka. When dry, use black edible pen or royal icing dyed black (see page 76) to add cute facial features and details to the paws.

STEP 8 ▼

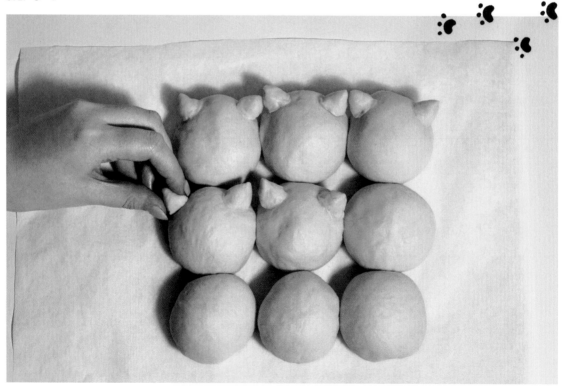

"Dough you may doubt yourself, remember the times, however small they might be, that you have risen to a challenge."

Tangzhong CATmembert & Honey Wreath

Yes. Not just warm, oozing camembert... this is CATmembert! This wreath is not only cute and pun-ful, it is also delicious and makes a great starter for everybody to share. Be warned: you will not want to stop eating this.

As camembert is extremely rich and full of fat, I prefer the bread I eat with it to be not so rich, so in my recipe I use the 'tangzhong' method. There is far less butter in tangzhong-style bread, but it is just as soft as brioche and incredibly addictive! I love the crust baked to this colour because it contrasts with the paleness of the camembert and is pretty striking. A bit of sweetness from the honey brushed on top gives it extra shine and pairs perfectly with the cheese.

What's great is that camembert and bread take about the same amount of time to bake, so it's all really straightforward!

SERVES: 6–8

TANGZHONG PASTE
25g [3 Tbsp] strong white [bread] flour, plus extra for dusting
100ml [⅓ cup plus 1 Tbsp] water

YEASTED DOUGH
160ml [⅔ cup] whole milk
50g [3½ Tbsp] unsalted butter

oil, for oiling
40g [3¼ Tbsp] caster or granulated sugar
1 tsp salt
1 large egg
420g [3 cups] strong white [bread] flour
7g [2¼ tsp] fast-action dried [active dry] yeast

CATS (NON-YEASTED DOUGH)
150g [1 cup plus 2 Tbsp] plain [all-purpose] flour
25ml [2 Tbsp] double [heavy] cream
60ml [¼ cup] water
pinch of salt

PLUS
food dyes or edible lustre dusts
a small amount of vodka or alcohol-based extract
1 camembert in its box
1 garlic clove, cut into thin slivers
fresh rosemary sprigs
1 egg, lightly beaten, for brushing
honey, for brushing

1 / First, make the tangzhong paste. Using a balloon whisk, mix the flour and water together in a pan until smooth. Place the pan over a low-medium heat and stir constantly with a spatula until thickened to a pudding-like consistency. If you have a thermometer, the paste should reach 65°C [149°F] before you take it off the heat. Transfer the tangzhong to a small bowl, cover with plastic wrap (making sure this touches the surface of the tangzhong) and chill in the freezer for 10 minutes.

2 / Meanwhile, for the yeasted dough, warm the milk in the microwave. It should be warm but not hot. Melt the butter, too. Lightly oil a large bowl and set aside.

3 / Place the milk and butter in a large bowl and add the sugar and salt. Add the chilled tangzhong to the bowl along with the egg and whisk together.

4 / Add the flour and yeast to the mixture. If using a stand mixer, just allow the machine to knead for 10 minutes with the dough hook attachment. If working by hand, use a wooden spoon to combine everything into a shaggy ball of dough, then turn out onto a floured surface. Knead by hand for about 10–15 minutes. The dough will be sticky to start with, but avoid adding too much flour – it will gradually become less sticky as you knead it. If the dough sticks to the surface, use a dough scraper to scrape it off. Keep kneading until the dough is smooth; it will still be a little tacky, but that is normal.

5 / Place the dough into a lightly oiled large bowl and cover with plastic wrap. Leave to rise in a warm place until doubled in size. This takes about 1 hour, but it depends on the temperature of your kitchen.

6 / While the dough is rising, make the non-yeasted dough. Preheat the oven to 180°C [350°F/Gas mark 4]. Place all the ingredients in a bowl and mix into a shaggy ball of dough. Turn out onto a work surface and knead until a smooth ball is formed.

7 / Use the dough to shape cats. You can make as few or as many as you like.

Sneak in a bear among the cats and you could call this recipe a CAT'n'BEAR!

8 / Paint facial details and markings onto the cats using food dyes or edible lustre dusts mixed with a little vodka for this (see picture below).

9 / Transfer the cats to a baking sheet and bake for 45 minutes. You may need to cover them with foil to prevent them browning. Leave to cool on a rack.

10 / When the yeasted dough has doubled in size, it is time to shape the bread. Divide the dough into 27 equal pieces.

I like to weigh the dough so that each piece is the same weight. It's a bit tedious, but I find that just using your eyes to judge size is often quite inaccurate! Weighing them ensures uniformity.

STEP 8 ▼

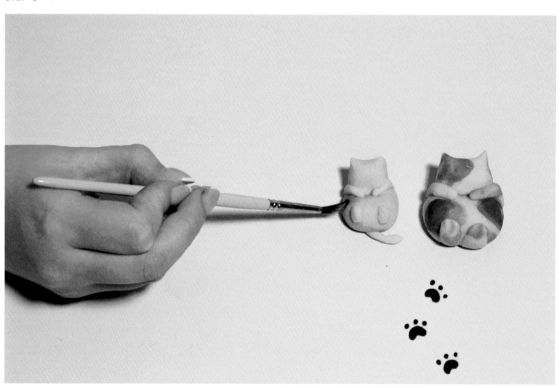

11 / Shape the pieces into round balls – try to get a smooth, taut surface on all of them to ensure a good oven spring. Arrange these around the camembert box (you can leave the actual camembert in the fridge for now): 9 in the inner ring and then 18 in the outer ring. Leave small gaps in between each bread bun, as they will expand and join when they rise. Loosely cover with lightly oiled plastic wrap and leave to prove in a warm place for about 1 hour, or until nearly doubled in size and the dough springs back halfway when lightly pressed with a finger.

12 / Meanwhile, preheat the oven to 180°C [350°F/ Gas mark 4]. Once the bread has risen, pop the camembert in its box and poke a few slivers of garlic and some rosemary sprigs into it. Brush the beaten egg over the bread and arrange the cats between the balls of dough, being careful not to deflate them (see picture above).

13 / Bake for about 20 minutes. The bread should be a deep golden brown colour, and the camembert should be liquid and bubbly inside.

14 / Remove from the oven and brush with honey immediately, then eat straightaway! (Be careful, the camembert will be very hot! I like to wait until it is slightly cooler and gooey.)

This bread is perfect for sharing, as it's round and you can tear off individual bits of bread… and cats! It is so satisfying and social, too!

Rustic No-knead Overnight Caraway Bread

Every baker needs a bread that they can make with little effort, and no-knead breads are the answer. Just roughly mix the ingredients in a large bowl the night before, cover, then in the morning shape, leave to rise and bake. Crusty, crackly and soft inside, you will have requests to make this bread over and over again!

Ideally, you will get the best springiness if you have a Dutch oven or cast-iron pan with a fitted lid. This will trap the steam and allow you to get a similar rise as a professional bread oven would give you, but all in your own home. Even if you don't have this equipment, you can't really go wrong with this bread!

"Similar to the beauty of a rustic loaf, you don't knead to be perfect to prove yourself."

MAKES: 1 MEDIUM LOAF

500g [3½ cups] strong
   white [bread] flour, plus
   extra for dusting

2 tsp caraway seeds
2g [½ tsp] fast-action dried
   [active dry] yeast

10g [2 tsp] salt
350ml [1½ cups] water
oil, for oiling

1 / Place the flour and caraway seeds in a bowl. Add the yeast to one side of the bowl, and the salt to the other, and use a spoon to mix together roughly.

2 / Pour in the water, then use a wooden spoon to mix into a rough ball and ensure there is no dry flour remaining. Cover with oiled plastic wrap and leave for about 8–10 hours, or overnight.

3 / In the morning, flour a banneton/proving basket or line a bowl with a well-floured linen cloth. Knock back the dough and shape into a round with a smooth surface and any seams/creases underneath. Place, seam-side up, into the prepared banneton or bowl for its second rise. If you can't shape your dough to be smooth, then don't worry about it! Your bread won't need scoring and will have a lovely rustic and crackled crust instead. Leave to prove at room temperature for 1–2 hours until almost doubled in size.

4 / Meanwhile, preheat the oven to its maximum temperature. It's also important to preheat the Dutch

oven for a good 45 minutes or so, but if you aren't using one, you can preheat a baking sheet instead.

5 / When the bread has finished its second rise, remove the Dutch oven, if using, from the oven and take off the lid (it will be extremely hot, so make sure you use really good oven gloves!). Carefully tip the bread into the hot Dutch oven. If you shaped your dough with a smooth surface, ideally you want to score it with a very sharp blade at this point. If your surface is rough, leave it as it is! Cover the Dutch oven with the lid and carefully place in the oven. If you are not using a Dutch oven, then tip your risen dough onto a flat tray or piece of stiff card lined with baking paper, then slide the bread (along with the paper) onto the hot baking sheet in the oven.

6 / Bake for 15 minutes, then uncover the Dutch oven at this point, if using, as this allows the crust to colour, turn the oven down to 220°C [425°F/Gas mark 7] and bake for a further 25 minutes. Bake for 40 minutes in total. Then carefully turn the bread onto a rack and leave to cool before eating!

Space Turtle Melonpan Buns

Melonpan is a classic Japanese sweet bread that is traditionally shaped to look like a melon; the name 'melonpan' refers to the appearance of the bread, not its flavour. The cookie-dough crust that makes it look like a melon is also what can make these look like turtles! People will love these not only for how cute they look, but also for the contrast of the crunchy and sweet top with the soft, fluffy interior.

You can leave this unfilled, which is how they traditionally are, or you can add a filling of your choice!

MAKES: 9

DOUGH
300g [2 cups plus 2 Tbsp] strong white [bread] flour, plus extra for dusting
20g [1½ Tbsp] caster or granulated sugar
6g [1 tsp] salt
7g [2¼ tsp] fast-action dried [active dry] yeast
30g [2 Tbsp] butter
70ml [⅓ cup] milk
1 medium egg
oil, for oiling
70ml [⅓ cup] water
1 egg, lightly beaten, for brushing

'SHELL'
50g [3½ Tbsp] salted butter, at room temperature
70g [⅓ cup] caster or granulated sugar, plus extra for sprinkling
1 medium egg, lightly beaten
160g [1¼ cups] plain [all-purpose] flour
¼ tsp bicarbonate of soda [baking soda]
1 tsp matcha (green tea) powder or drop of green food dye

OPTIONAL FILLINGS
chocolate or red or black bean paste (you can buy this from most Chinese supermarkets)

SILVER STAR & MOON DECORATIONS
white sugarpaste
a small amount of vodka or alcohol-based extract
edible glitter
black edible pen or Royal Icing (see page 76), dyed black

1 / Place the flour, sugar, salt, and yeast in a large bowl. Heat the butter in the microwave until melted, then heat the milk in another heatproof bowl in the microwave until warm but not hot to the touch. Beat the egg in a separate bowl. Lightly oil a large bowl and set aside.

2 / Add the melted butter, warm milk, water and 2 Tbsp of the beaten egg to the dry mixture. If using a stand mixer, just allow the machine to knead for 10 minutes with the dough hook attachment. If working by hand, use a wooden spoon to combine everything into a shaggy ball of dough, then turn out onto a floured surface.

3 / Knead by hand for about 10–15 minutes. The dough will be sticky to start with, but avoid adding too much flour – it will gradually become less sticky as you knead it. If the dough sticks to the surface, use a dough scraper to scrape it off. Keep kneading until the dough is smooth; it will still be a little tacky, but that is normal.

4 / Place the dough into the oiled bowl and cover with plastic wrap. Leave to rise at room temperature until it has doubled in size. This takes about an hour, but it depends on the temperature of your kitchen.

5 / When the dough has doubled in size, turn it out onto a lightly floured surface and knock back. Shape 9 balls of dough, each weighing 45g [1½oz]. Shape them by tucking the dough under to create a smooth surface. These will form the main body of the turtle. At this point, you can also add a filling into the middle, such as chocolate. Just make sure you carefully wrap the dough around the filling so that it is encased in the centre. There will be some leftover dough – this is to shape the heads and legs.

6 / Weigh out 10g [¼oz] of dough for the head of each turtle, shape into a ball, then attach it to the body. Repeat for all 9 turtles. Shape the remaining dough into small balls and attach to the sides of the turtle to create its feet (see picture below).

7 / Cover with lightly oiled plastic wrap and leave to rise for about 45 minutes (but this varies depending on the temperature of your kitchen). It is ready when you poke it gently with a floured finger and it springs back halfway. The impression should not stay or spring back straightaway.

8 / Meanwhile, make the cookie-dough 'shell'. Cream the butter and sugar together in a bowl, then mix in the egg. Add the flour, bicarbonate of soda and matcha powder or green food dye and mix until it forms a ball. Wrap in plastic wrap.

9 / Towards the end of the rise, preheat the oven to 170°C [340°F/Gas mark 3]. When the dough has risen and is ready to bake, roll out the cookie dough on a lightly floured surface and stamp out 9 x 9-cm [3½-in] circles for the turtles' backs. Sprinkle caster sugar over these. Brush the bread dough with the beaten egg before adding the cookie-dough circles to form the turtles' shells. Score the shells in a criss-cross pattern using a very sharp knife. Bake for 20 minutes until lightly golden brown. You may need to cover the bread with foil after 5–10 minutes to prevent it from browning too much.

10 / Transfer to a rack to cool completely.

STEP 6 ▼

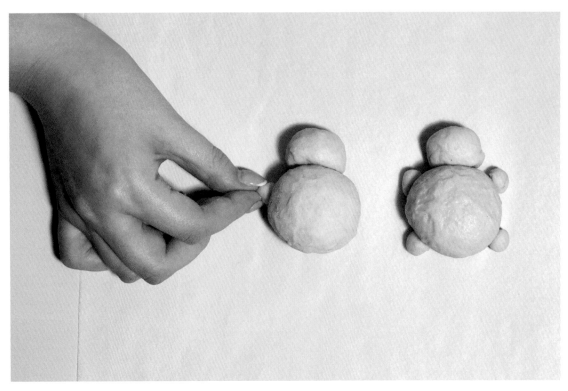

11 / Meanwhile, make the silver moons and stars. Roll out the sugarpaste, and use a cutter (or hand-cut using a knife) to create star and moon shapes. Place these on a baking sheet lined with greaseproof paper. To harden the sugarpaste, make sure the oven is off and has cooled a bit (leave the oven door open to speed this up), before placing the sheet of shapes in. Check every few minutes to make sure the shapes are not melting (if so the oven is too hot!) or drying out excessively. When hardened, brush the fondant shapes with a little vodka and use a paintbrush to cover with edible glitter.

12 / When the bread is fully cool, add the facial features using edible black pen or royal icing dyed black (see page 76). Add edible star sprinkles and the glittered star/moon shapes using edible glue (or royal icing) to adhere.

"It's OK to need your own space to reflect sometimes. It's often the star-t of an out-of-this-world idea!"

Square Cakes

Firework Cake

Parkin cake is traditionally made for Bonfire Night in the UK, so decorating this cake with colourful fireworks really fits the theme! Whether you decorate it on this theme or not, this cake is deliciously gingery and gets even better over a few days. It will become stickier and even more decadent.

SERVES: 16

250g [1 cup plus 2 Tbsp] unsalted butter, plus extra for greasing
¼ tsp salt
200g [⅔ cup] golden [light corn] syrup
80g [¼ cup] black treacle [molasses]
100g [½ cup] dark muscovado [soft brown] sugar

1 large egg
60ml [¼ cup] milk
100g [1 cup] porridge oats
250g [1¾ cups plus 2 Tbsp] self-raising [self-rising] flour
1½ Tbsp ground ginger
60g [2oz] crystallized stem [candied preserved] ginger, finely chopped

TO DECORATE
¼ quantity of either Italian Meringue Buttercream (see page 64) or American Buttercream (see page 60)
¾ tsp vanilla bean paste
dark blue food dye
edible glitter
½ quantity of Royal Icing (see page 76)

yellow, purple, blue, orange and pink food dyes

1 / Preheat the oven to 140°C [275°F/Gas mark 1]. Grease a 23-cm [9-in] square baking tin and line the base with baking paper.

2 / Melt the butter with the salt, golden syrup, treacle and sugar in a pan over a medium heat, stirring until all the butter has melted.

3 / In a small bowl, whisk the egg and milk together. Add it to the pan and whisk to combine.

4 / Mix the oats, flour, ground ginger and finely chopped crystallized ginger together in separate bowl, then pour in the liquid mixture from the pan and whisk until just combined.

5 / Pour the mixture into the prepared cake tin and bake for 1 hour, or until a knife inserted into the centre comes out clean.

6 / Run a knife around the sides of the cake and turn out onto a rack. You can leave the cake to cool, then cut into squares and serve, or decorate it.

7 / While the cake is cooling, make your choice of buttercream for the decoration, flavour with the vanilla bean paste and colour with dark blue dye.

8 / When the cake is cool, cover with a thin layer of the buttercream and sprinkle with some edible glitter. Chill the cake in the fridge while you make the royal icing to a pipeable consistency (see page 76).

9 / Divide the royal icing among 6 bowls. Keep one bowl white, then dye the others as follows: yellow, purple, blue, orange and pink. Transfer each colour to a piping bag and snip a small tip.

10 / Pipe lines and dots onto the cake using different colours to create a colourful firework display!

Royal icing won't harden completely when piped on top of buttercream, but it is so much easier to pipe thin lines with royal icing than with buttercream!

Create your own firework display – just have a look at photographs for inspiration!

Lavender & Orange Cake

This delicious flavour combination is the perfect base for paintings using buttercream. Buttercream is lovely to work with because you can easily create texture and pops of colours. Also, unlike proper paint, if anything goes wrong you can just scrape it off and eat it! Try creating your own designs – you can paint most things that you would on paper or canvas. Try more floral designs or a beautiful sunset over the sea, or even your own self-portrait!

SERVES: 16

1¼ tsp culinary lavender buds

180g [¾ cup plus 2 tsp] unsalted butter, at room temperature, cubed, plus extra for greasing

180g [1 scant cup] caster or granulated sugar

¼ tsp salt

180g [6oz] shelled eggs (about 5 large)

½ tsp vanilla bean paste

220g [1⅔ cups] self-raising [self-rising] flour

60ml [¼ cup] whole milk

ORANGE BUTTERCREAM

¼ quantity of Italian Meringue Buttercream (see page 64), plus grated zest of ¾ orange

AUTUMNAL DESIGN

blue, yellow, orange, red, brown and green food dyes

a small amount of vodka or alcohol-based extract

FLORAL DESIGN

orange, green, pink, purple and yellow food dyes

edible white pearl sprinkles (or similar)

1 / Preheat the oven to 180°C [350°F/Gas mark 4]. Grease a 23-cm [9-in] square baking tin and line the base with baking paper. Add the lavender buds to a mortar and pestle and grind by hand just to soften and break up the buds. Set aside.

2 / Add the butter, sugar and salt to a stand mixer (or use a handheld electric whisk) fitted with the balloon whisk attachment and beat on medium speed until the butter is smooth. Increase the speed to high and beat until the butter is fluffy and pale in colour.

3 / Lightly beat the eggs in a separate bowl. Add the eggs, 1 Tbsp at a time, to the creamed butter and sugar mixture, beating well after each addition. Add the lavender and vanilla bean paste and mix to combine.

4 / Add the flour and milk and continue mixing on low speed until just combined.

5 / Spoon the mixture into the prepared tin and bake for 30–40 minutes until a knife inserted into the centre comes out clean.

6 / While the cake is baking, make the Italian meringue buttercream following the recipe on page 64. Just make a quarter of the recipe and flavour with the orange zest.

7 / When the cake is baked, run a knife around the edges and turn out onto a rack. Peel off the baking paper and leave the cake to cool completely before covering with the buttercream.

Turn over for instructions on creating an autumnal cake (see picture opposite) or a floral one!

FOR THE AUTUMNAL DESIGN

1 / Dye a small amount of the buttercream a pale blue colour. Spread this over the cake and smooth. Chill in the fridge.

2 / While the buttercream chills, divide the remaining buttercream among 5 bowls. Dye the buttercream in each of the bowls the following colours: yellow, orange, red, brown and green. Add a very small amount of brown food dye to the yellow, orange and red to make these colours more autumnal.

3 / First, apply the brown buttercream with a palette knife to form the main shape of the tree trunks and larger branches in the foreground on top of the cake. Use a tiny bit of brown food dye mixed with a small amount of vodka to paint the smaller details like tiny branches coming off, and the small trees in the distance. Use a palette knife or paintbrush to apply dots of different-coloured buttercream onto the trees, and smooth together. Apply different-coloured buttercreams together to create the ground. Finally, use buttercream to create the shape of a figure in the distance.

FOR THE FLORAL DESIGN

1 / Spread a thin and smooth layer of the buttercream over the cake, then chill in the fridge.

2 / While the buttercream chills, divide the remaining buttercream among 5 bowls. Leave 1 bowl white and dye the remaining 4 the following colours: green, pink, purple and yellow.

3 / Use palette knives (the ones you would use with oil paint) to apply buttercream on top of the cake to look like flowers (see picture below). Use different colours and overlap some flowers, then create leaves using the green buttercream. Use a paintbrush to feather the centre of each flower outwards, then add pearl sprinkles to the centres for the flower eyes.

"Give yourself the chance to bloom – you will in time."

STEP 3 ▼ **FLORAL DESIGN**

Lady Lemon Drizzle Cake

This soft and moist lemon drizzle cake is full of flavour, as there is lemon zest in the cake. It is then soaked with lemon syrup when it comes out of the oven and taken a step FURTHER with a lemon glaze. And not just that, Lady Lemon insists on the presence of gorgeously candied fruit on top. She is the queen of lemons after all, and only the best cake will do.

SERVES: 16

180g [¾ cup plus 2 tsp] unsalted butter, at room temperature, cubed, plus extra for greasing
180g [1 scant cup] caster or granulated sugar
¼ tsp salt
180g [6oz] shelled eggs (about 5 large)
grated zest of 2 large lemons

½ tsp vanilla bean paste
220g [1⅔ cups] self-raising [self-rising] flour
60ml [¼ cup] whole milk

LEMON SIMPLE SYRUP
80g [⅓ cup] caster or granulated sugar
120ml [½ cup] lemon juice

LEMON GLAZE
210g [1½ cups] icing [confectioners'] sugar
2½ Tbsp lemon juice

CANDIED FRUIT
1 lemon
1 orange
190ml [¾ cup] water
2 Tbsp lemon juice

200g [1 cup] caster or granulated sugar

ROYAL ICING (TO PIPE FACE PROFILE)
½ quantity of Royal ilcing (see page 76)
brown food dye

PLUS
edible gold leaf

1 / Preheat the oven to 180°C [350°F/Gas mark 4]. Grease a 23-cm [9-in] square baking tin and line the base with baking paper.

2 / Add the butter, sugar and salt to a stand mixer (or use a handheld electric whisk) fitted with the balloon whisk attachment and beat on medium speed until the butter is smooth. Increase the heat to high and beat until the butter is fluffy and pale in colour.

3 / Lightly beat the eggs in a separate bowl. Add the eggs, 1 Tbsp at a time, to the creamed butter and sugar mixture, beating well after each addition. Add the lemon zest and vanilla bean paste and mix to combine.

4 / Add the flour and milk and mix on low speed until just combined.

5 / Spoon the mixture into the prepared tin and bake for 30–40 minutes until a knife inserted into the centre comes out clean.

6 / While the cake is baking, make the lemon simple syrup. Heat all the ingredients in a small pan over a medium heat, stirring occasionally, until the mixture comes to a simmer. Simmer for 2 minutes, then take off the heat.

7 / When the cake is baked, run a knife around the edges and turn out onto a rack. Peel off the baking paper.

8 / Immediately poke holes all over the surface of the cake and use a pastry brush to soak the cake with all the lemon simple syrup, then leave to cool.

9 / Meanwhile, make the lemon glaze. Whisk the icing sugar and lemon juice together in a bowl until there are no lumps.

10 / When the cake is only slightly warm to the touch, spread on the lemon glaze. Use a warm, sharp knife to neatly trim off the edges of the cake, then transfer to a serving plate.

STEP 12 ▼

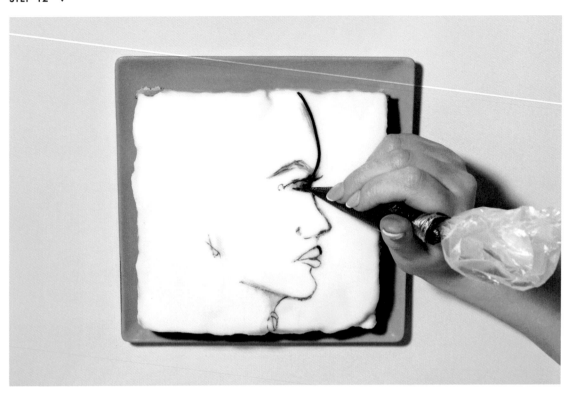

STEP 13 ▼

- SQUARE CAKES -

11 / While you wait for the glaze to set, make the candied fruit slices. Slice the lemon and orange into 3-mm [⅛-in] thick slices, discarding the seeds. Add the water, lemon juice and sugar to a shallow pan and simmer, stirring occasionally, until the sugar has dissolved. Add the lemon and orange slices and simmer for another 15 minutes, turning them occasionally, until the rinds are soft and the fruit is translucent. Transfer to a sheet of baking paper and leave to cool.

12 / Next, make the royal icing (see page 76). Add the brown food dye to colour, then transfer to a piping bag. Snip a small tip and use to pipe the profile of Lady Lemon's face, now that the glaze is set with a crust (see picture opposite, above). To help guide you, you can first paint a guide using brown food dye mixed with a little water.

13 / Arrange the candied lemon and orange slices to decorate, then add edible gold leaf (see picture opposite, below).

YOU CAN EASILY MAKE THIS CAKE VEGAN!

DRY INGREDIENTS
250g [1¾ cups plus 2 Tbsp] self-raising [self-rising] flour
180g [1 scant cup] caster or granulated sugar
grated zest of 2 large lemons
2½ tsp baking powder

WET INGREDIENTS
coconut oil or vegan spread, for oiling
1¼ tsp white wine vinegar
280ml [1 cup plus 3 Tbsp] soy milk
110ml [7½ Tbsp] sunflower oil or other
   neutral-tasting oil
2½ tsp aquafaba (see page 30)
1 tsp vanilla bean paste

1 / Preheat the oven to 170°C [340°F/Gas mark 3]. Oil a 23-cm [9-in] square baking tin with coconut oil or vegan spread and line the base with baking paper.

2 / In a large bowl, combine all the dry ingredients.

3 / For the wet ingredients, in a separate bowl, mix the vinegar with the soy milk in a large bowl until it curdles and thickens. Add the rest of the wet ingredients and stir together.

4 / Add the dry ingredients to the wet and whisk until just combined. Pour the mixture straightaway into the prepared tin and bake for 25–30 minutes until a knife inserted into the centre comes out clean.

5 / Follow the same steps as the main recipe with the syrup, glaze and candied fruit. Use the vegan version of the royal icing recipe on page 76 for the piping work.

Little Bakes

Macaron Tips & Ideas

I use the Italian meringue method for making macarons, as I find it is less temperamental and it doesn't take much longer to prepare. The method is similar to the Italian Meringue Buttercream on page 64. Ideally, you do need a stand mixer for these, as it involves multitasking – whisking egg whites at high speed while pouring hot sugar onto them. You will also need a sugar thermometer for the sugar syrup. But these things are worth it for a beautiful macaron!

Macarons are tricky, so don't be disheartened if they don't work out the first time. Expect to try a few times before you get them right! Here are some helpful tips:

• Make sure your almonds are ground up very finely. I find that shop-bought ground almonds in the UK are not fine enough, so I process them in a spice grinder just for a few seconds (not TOO long, otherwise they release their oils and turn into nut butter), then sift the ground almonds to remove any larger pieces.

• It helps to have an oven thermometer, and not to have oven hotspots for an even bake! An oven thermometer helps, as sometimes your oven is not the temperature you think it is, and macarons are so sensitive to oven temperature.

• I recommend a flat surface and a macaron template. I used to pipe my macarons on baking paper, which does work, but you just need to make sure it is very flat and preferably without any creases. If it isn't, then some of your macarons might become misshapen. I now prefer to use a non-stick silicone baking mat because this won't crease. You can place any template or guides underneath the silicone mat, as they are slightly see-through. You can also buy silicone mats with circle markings to guide you when piping.

• When piping, pipe from straight above rather than at an angle. This helps to achieve a round and even shape.

• Don't skip banging the baking sheet on the work surface – this is important to get any large air bubbles out. If you don't, they may expand and cause the macaron surface to crack!

• Give the macarons time to rest and form a skin! You can chill out and enjoy a break while they do. Again, this helps them to form their distinctive crinkly 'feet' and not crack on the surface.

• My Italian meringue macarons don't need folding for as long as French macarons do. Once you can lift the spatula and the mixture falls down like a ribbon, and you can form a figure-of-eight on the mixture, don't fold any more. It is always better to underfold than overfold. Remember that as you transfer the batter to the piping bag, you are essentially folding it further.

Macarons

MAKES: about 20 macarons

115g [½ cup plus 1¼ Tbsp] caster [superfine] sugar
40ml [2⅔ Tbsp] water

MIXTURE A
105g [1 cup] finely ground and sifted almonds

105g [¾ cup plus 1½ Tbsp] sifted icing [confectioners'] sugar
40g [1½oz] egg white (or aquafaba [see opposite])

MIXTURE B
45g [1½oz] egg whites, at room temperature (or aquafaba [see opposite])

1 / First, line 2 baking sheets with baking paper or a silicone mat. Have any templates ready to hand and organized. Also have all your piping bags and any food dyes you will be using ready to hand.

2 / For Mixture A, stir the sifted ground almonds and icing sugar together in a large bowl. Add the egg white (or aquafaba) and mix until it forms a paste.

3 / Add Mixture B to a stand mixer (or use a handheld electric whisk) fitted with the balloon whisk attachment.

4 / Add the caster sugar and water to a pan and stir occasionally over a medium-high heat until the sugar has dissolved and the mixture starts to bubble. Start whisking the egg white (or aquafaba) to soft peaks. You want to time the sugar syrup reaching 115°C [239°F] with the egg whites (or aquafaba) reaching soft peaks. You can always take the sugar syrup off the stove and/or slow the mixer (but don't turn it off) to time the two together.

The aquafaba will take longer to whisk to soft peaks than the egg white, so bear this in mind when timing this with the sugar syrup reaching 115°C [239°F].

5 / When the egg whites (or aquafaba) have reached soft peaks and the sugar syrup is at 115°C [239°F], raise the speed of the mixer (or whisk) to high while pouring the sugar syrup in a thin stream down the side of the bowl (do not pour directly onto the whisk).

6 / Once all the sugar has been poured in, continue whisking on high speed until the side of the bowl feels cool to the touch, 3–5 minutes or so. At this point, turn off the mixer and use a spatula to fold the meringue into Mixture A. Add food dye to colour. If using multiple colours, distribute the macaron mixture between bowls and colour each individually before transferring to piping bags.

7 / Pipe the macarons onto the prepared baking sheets or mat (and templates, if using). If the macaron mixture is the correct consistency, the macarons should spread slightly after piping but still hold their shape, and the tip of the macarons should disappear within a minute or so.

8 / After piping, pick up the baking sheet or mat and bang it on a flat surface about 3 times. You should see air bubbles come to the surface. Some of them might pop of their own accord, but you might have to use a cocktail stick [toothpick] to help pop a few (which is very satisfying!).

9 / Leave the macarons for at least 1–2 hours to form a skin on the surface – you should be able to gently touch the macaron and it shouldn't come away on your finger. The time it takes for the macarons to form a skin depends on how humid the air is, so it could take longer.

VEGAN MACARON TIPS

If you're making these macarons vegan, it's easy! Follow the main recipe but just switch the egg white for aquafaba – and it's best if you can reduce the aquafaba beforehand so that its consistency is similar to egg whites (see below). You also need to bake the vegan version at a lower temperature for longer, as they are more sensitive to heat, but other than that, the same rules apply to both!

To reduce down aquafaba, you will need 85g [⅓ cup] aquafaba in total. So start with 170g [¾ cup] aquafaba (the liquid drained from a can of chickpeas [garbanzo beans]) and pour this into a pan. Simmer over a medium heat until you have 85–90g [¾ cup] aquafaba remaining. You will need to estimate when it's reduced by about half and then weigh it. If it isn't quite there, give it a little more time and then re-weigh. Leave the aquafaba to cool to room temperature before using in the recipe. This stuff doesn't look particularly appetizing, but have faith – it does work!

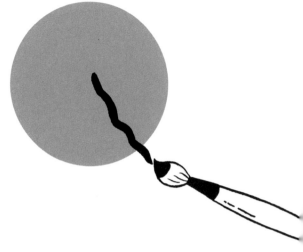

10 / When the macarons are ready, preheat the oven to 150°C [300°F/Gas mark 2] (or 120°C [250°F/Gas mark ½] for vegan macarons). Bake the egg white-based macarons for about 15 minutes (the vegan macarons for 30 minutes).

11 / Leave the macarons to cool before peeling them off the baking paper and then filling (and decorating). They are best chilled in the fridge for a day or so before serving, as this helps to soften the shell – this is especially the case for the vegan macarons because they tend to be crunchier due to their longer baking time.

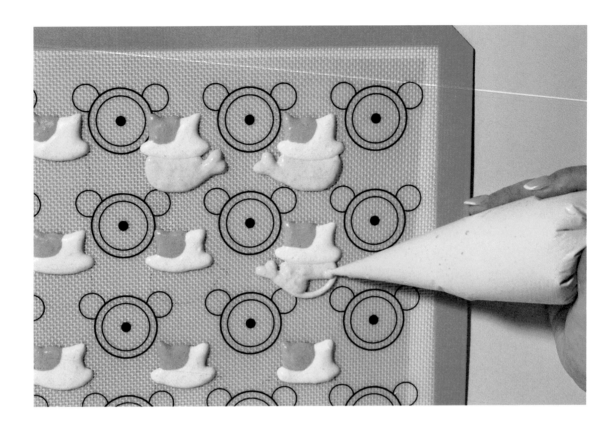

TO MAKE PURRMAIDS

Before making your macaron mixture, first draw out a template on a piece of card and cut out. Draw around this several times on a piece of paper or card (making sure to reverse it half the time, otherwise your purrmaids' tails won't align when you sandwich them together!), and slide this under your silicone mat or baking paper so that it can be used as a guide.

Next, make your macaron mixture, divide it among 3 bowls and colour as follows: white, grey and blue or pink. Transfer to 3 piping bags and cut a small tip.

Pipe the macaron mixture carefully between the lines, starting with all the heads (grey and white batter) and then adding the tails at the end. After piping, tap the baking sheet on a flat surface, as you would do normally.

After baking and cooling, draw in the faces on the purrmaids using an edible black pen, then add the blush using edible pink lustre dust applied with a paintbrush. Paint the patterns onto the tails using edible silver and gold paint.

- LITTLE BAKES -

TO MAKE CATS

Make your macaron mixture. Spoon out 4 Tbsp of mixture and divide between 2 bowls. Colour one bowl brown and the other pink. Colour the main bowl of mixture yellow. Transfer the yellow mixture to a piping bag fitted with a large round piping nozzle [tip]. Transfer the other colours to small piping bags and set aside for now.

Use the yellow piping bag to pipe circular yellow macarons. Pipe these at a 90-degree angle to the baking sheet. When there is a small amount of mixture left, cut the nozzle off the piping bag, then slip the bag into a new one and cut a small opening.

Create the cats' ears using this smaller tip: squeeze the piping bag at a 45-degree angle from the round macaron shape, then gradually squeeze with less pressure to form a point (on just half the macarons, as the other half will have tails!). At this point, tap the sheet on a flat surface and leave the macarons to form a skin. When the skin has formed, add the tails (use the remainder of the yellow batter) and the face detailing (brown and pink batters – just snip a small tip). After baking and cooling, draw in the finer black details using an edible ink pen.

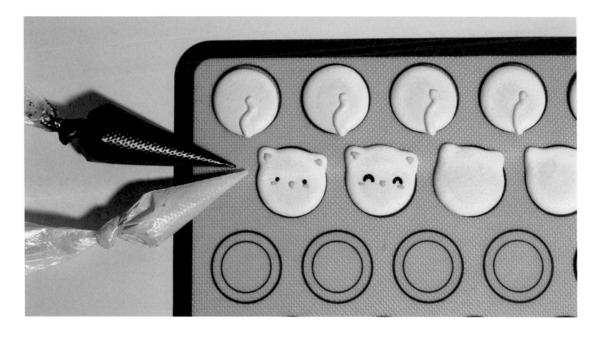

- LITTLE BAKES -

- LITTLE BAKES -

White Ganache for Macarons

There are so many ways to flavour this ganache: pistachio paste, liqueurs, almond extract, coffee, freeze-dried raspberry/strawberry/blueberry powder, orange zest, rosewater, ground cardamom, etc. Add your flavours gradually – tasting as you go along – while whisking the chocolate but before it has thickened, or infuse in the heated cream or coconut milk (this is better for ingredients like cardamom and orange zest).

MAKES: ENOUGH TO FILL ABOUT 20 MACARONS

WHITE CHOCOLATE GANACHE
110g [3¾oz] white chocolate
70ml [⅓ cup minus 2 tsp] double [heavy] cream

VEGAN WHITE CHOCOLATE GANACHE
110g [3¾oz] vegan white chocolate
70ml [⅓ cup] coconut milk

VEGAN WHITE CHOCOLATE GANACHE ALTERNATIVE
(this is delicious and creamy when you don't have vegan white chocolate to hand)
50g [¼ cup] cocoa butter
25g [2 Tbsp] coconut oil
65g [½ cup] icing [confectioners'] sugar
50ml [3⅓ Tbsp] coconut milk

1a / If using solid chocolate pieces, chop it into small, roughly equal pieces and add it to a bowl.

2a / Pour the cream or coconut milk into a pan and bring to a simmer over a medium-high heat. When it starts to bubble, pour it on top of the chocolate. Make sure the cream covers all the chocolate pieces and leave for 3 minutes.

3a / After 3 minutes, stir to combine all the cream or coconut milk and chocolate. The chocolate should be completely melted by now. If not, pour it back into a pan and gently heat until the chocolate has melted.

4 / Add the mixture to a bowl, cover with plastic wrap and set aside until cooled to room temperature. Whisk until lightened in colour and the right thickness for filling macarons. While whisking, add any desired flavouring (see above). The ganache will take a little while to thicken, but it will reach a point and suddenly start to thicken quite quickly, so avoid overwhipping, as it will become too difficult to pipe. Transfer to a piping bag and use to fill your macarons.

1b / If you don't have vegan white chocolate and are looking for a vegan white chocolate ganache filling, put the cocoa butter and coconut oil in a pan and melt over a low heat.

2b / Pour into a bowl and add the icing sugar, then whisk until smooth.

3b / Add the coconut milk and continue whisking until the mixture becomes whiter in colour, fluffy and a pipeable consistency. While whisking, you can add your desired flavourings (see above). The mixture will take a while to thicken, so be patient. It helps to use a stand mixer fitted with a whisk attachment, as you will need to whisk it for at least 5 minutes, but otherwise use a handheld electric whisk. Transfer to a piping bag and use to fill your macarons.

Dark Ganache for Macarons

You can flavour this ganache by adding a little liqueur (e.g. amaretto), almond extract, other flavouring oils, ground cardamom or orange zest. Or make a praline paste (see page 15) and mix in, to add another dimension. Also try adding a little salt. Add these to the chocolate when melted but before it has set, or infuse into the heated cream or coconut milk (this is better for ingredients like cardamom and orange zest).

MAKES: ENOUGH TO FILL ABOUT 20 MACARONS

DARK CHOCOLATE GANACHE
80g [2¾oz] dark chocolate (at least 70% cocoa solids)
80ml [⅓ cup] double [heavy] cream
20g [2¼ Tbsp] icing [confectioners'] sugar, or to taste (optional, as this depends on the sweetness of your dark chocolate)

VEGAN DARK CHOCOLATE GANACHE
80g [2¾oz] vegan dark chocolate
80ml [⅓ cup] coconut milk
20g [2¼ Tbsp] icing [confectioners'] sugar, or to taste (optional, as this depends on the sweetness of your dark chocolate)

1 / Chop the chocolate into small, roughly equal pieces, then add to a bowl.

2 / Pour the cream or coconut milk into a pan and bring to a simmer over a medium-high heat. When it starts to bubble, pour it on top of the chocolate. Make sure the cream covers all the chocolate pieces and leave for 3 minutes.

3 / After 3 minutes, stir to combine all the cream or coconut milk and chocolate. The chocolate should be completely melted by now. If not, pour it back into a pan and gently heat until the chocolate has melted. Stir in the sugar, if using.

4 / Add the mixture to a bowl, cover with plastic wrap and set aside until cooled to room temperature. Whisk until lightened in colour and the right thickness for filling your macarons. While whisking, add any desired flavouring (see above). The ganache will take a little while to thicken, but it will reach a point and suddenly start to thicken quite quickly, so avoid overwhipping, as it will become too difficult to pipe. Transfer to a piping bag and use to fill your macarons.

"Spend some koala-ty time and make me with friends."

Orange Curd for Macarons

MAKES: ENOUGH TO FILL ABOUT 20 MACARONS

2 egg yolks
grated zest and juice of
  1 large orange (about
  100ml [7 Tbsp])

100g [½ cup] caster or
  granulated sugar
60g [¼ cup] unsalted
  butter

1 / Add the egg yolks, orange zest and juice, sugar and butter to a heatproof bowl and stir with a balloon whisk until combined.

2 / Set up a bain-marie with a pan of hot water on the stove, and the heatproof bowl fitting on top but without directly touching the water.

3 / Whisk constantly for 10–15 minutes until the mixture has thickened (you will notice the foam start to disappear) and holds a trail.

4 / Pour the curd into a bowl, cover with plastic wrap (touching the surface to avoid forming a skin) and chill in the fridge before using to fill your macarons. You can strain the curd before transferring to a bowl if you have any bits of cooked egg, or if you prefer not to have the zest.

Vegan Orange Curd for Macarons

MAKES: ENOUGH TO FILL ABOUT 20 MACARONS

grated zest and juice of
  1 large orange (about
  100ml [7 Tbsp])
100g [½ cup] caster or
  granulated sugar

1¼ Tbsp arrowroot powder
  or cornflour [cornstarch]
30ml [2 Tbsp] coconut milk
40g [¼ cup] coconut oil

1 / Combine the orange zest and juice, sugar and arrowroot or cornflour in a small pan. Stir constantly over a medium heat until the mixture thickens and coats the back of a spoon.

2 / Take off the heat, then immediately add the coconut milk and coconut oil. Stir in until completely melted and combined.

3 / Pour the mixture into a bowl and cover with plastic wrap (making sure it touches the surface of the curd to avoid it forming a film). Chill the bowl in the freezer for 1 hour before using to fill your macarons. It won't seem very thick initially, but will thicken to the perfect consistency as it cools.

Lemon Curd for Macarons

MAKES: ENOUGH TO FILL ABOUT 20 MACARONS

2 egg yolks
grated zest and juice of
  2 lemons (about 100ml
  [7 Tbsp])

110g [½ cup plus 1 Tbsp]
  caster or granulated
  sugar
60g [¼ cup] unsalted
  butter

1 / Add the egg yolks, orange zest and juice, sugar and butter to a heatproof bowl and stir with a balloon whisk until combined.

2 / Set up a bain-marie with a pan of hot water on the stove, and the heatproof bowl fitting on top but without directly touching the water.

3 / Whisk constantly for 10–15 minutes until the mixture has thickened (you will notice the foam start to disappear) and holds a trail.

4 / Pour the curd into a bowl, cover with plastic wrap (touching the surface to avoid forming a skin) and chill in the fridge before using to fill your macarons. You can strain the curd before transferring to a bowl if you have any bits of cooked egg, or if you prefer not to have the zest.

Vegan Lemon Curd for Macarons

MAKES: ENOUGH TO FILL ABOUT 20 MACARONS

grated zest and juice of
  2 lemons (about 100ml
  [7 Tbsp])
110g [½ cup plus 1 Tbsp]
  caster or granulated
  sugar

1¼ Tbsp arrowroot powder
  or cornflour [cornstarch]
30ml [2 Tbsp] coconut milk
40g [¼ cup] coconut oil

1 / Combine the lemon zest and juice, sugar and arrowroot or cornflour in a small pan. Stir constantly over a medium heat until the mixture thickens and coats the back of a spoon.

2 / Take off the heat, then immediately add the coconut milk and coconut oil. Stir in until completely melted and combined.

3 / Pour the mixture into a bowl and cover with plastic wrap (making sure it touches the surface of the curd to avoid it forming a film). Chill the bowl in the freezer for 1 hour before using to fill your macarons. It won't seem very thick initially, but will thicken to the perfect consistency as it cools.

Cardamom, Almond & Honey Bee Cookies

BZZZZZZ these will make you bee-come an instant hit at parties, as they're super cute but not cute enough not to be gobbled up! They look like they're a bit of an effort to make (yet they're so easy), so no one will think you're winging it!

MAKES: ABOUT 30

CARDAMOM COOKIES
Semolina Shortbread (see page 74) or Basic Vegan Shortbread (see page 75), plus ¾ tsp ground cardamom (for the best flavour, finely grind the seeds in a spice grinder)
yellow gel food dye

plain [all-purpose] flour, for dusting

BUTTERCREAM
75g [⅓ cup] butter, at room temperature (or vegetable shortening or coconut oil to make vegan)

125g [¾ cup plus 2 Tbsp] icing [confectioners'] sugar
½ tsp vanilla bean paste
1–2 Tbsp milk or plant-based milk, to soften as necessary

ROYAL ICING
½ quantity of Royal Icing (see page 76)
black gel food dye

PLUS
honey, or a thick maple syrup or agave syrup to make vegan
flaked [slivered] almonds

1 / Line 2 baking sheets with baking paper.

2 / Make the shortbread (see pages 74 or 75), adding the cardamom along with the flour. Add a little yellow food dye to colour the shortbread, if you like.

3 / Roll out the shortbread on a lightly floured surface to about 3mm [⅛ in] thick, and use a 4-cm [1½-in] diameter round cutter to stamp out about 60 cookies.

4 / Place these on the prepared baking sheets and preferably chill in the fridge or freezer for 30 minutes.

5 / Preheat the oven to 180°C [350°F/Gas mark 4] and bake the cookies for 10–15 minutes until just starting to colour at the edges.

6 / Meanwhile, make the buttercream. Put the butter and sugar in a large bowl, then cream together until light and fluffy. Add the vanilla bean paste and mix. Add the milk to soften to a pipeable consistency, and mix well to create a fluffy buttercream.

7 / When the cookies have finished baking, leave to cool on the baking sheet for 5 minutes before transferring them to a rack to finish cooling.

8 / While the cookies are cooling, make the royal icing (see page 76). Colour the royal icing black and transfer to a piping bag. Cut a small tip and set aside for later.

9 / When the cookies have cooled, you are ready to sandwich them together and decorate. Pipe buttercream around the circumference of a cookie disc, then spoon in a little honey (or maple or agave syrup) in the centre. The buttercream will stop the honey leaking out! Repeat with half the discs, then sandwich with the other discs.

10 / Pipe 3 black stripes on all the bees' bodies. Place the piping bag into another piping bag, and cut a smaller tip to pipe the finer details of the eyes and mouth. Insert flaked almonds into the buttercream on the sides to create the bees' wings.

White Chocolate & Orange Lady Choux

These elegant ladies with their little hats and arms will bring a smile to your face. You can also change the colours to a loved one's favourites, and make them a special gift. Crème diplomate-filled choux pastry is also a timeless combination that everyone will love. The filling is intentionally not too sweet, to pair perfectly with the sweet craquelin and marzipan.

MAKES: 20–24

ORANGE CRAQUELIN

75g [⅓ cup] unsalted butter
75g [6 Tbsp] light muscovado [soft brown] sugar
grated zest of 1 orange
75g [½ cup plus 1 Tbsp] plain [all-purpose] flour

ORANGE CREME DIPLOMATE

400ml [1¾ cups] whole milk
grated zest of 3 oranges
¾ tsp vanilla bean paste
7 large egg yolks

90g [scant ½ cup] caster or granulated sugar
60g [7¼ Tbsp] cornflour [cornstarch]
3–3½ Tbsp orange liqueur, to taste
170ml [¾ cup] double [heavy] cream

MARZIPAN (OPTIONAL)

125g [¾ cup plus 2 Tbsp] icing [confectioners'] sugar, plus extra for dusting
125g [1¼ cups] finely ground almonds
1 pasteurized egg white (or 35g [1¼oz])

¼ tsp almond extract
¾ tsp amaretto
blue food dye

CHOCOLATE HATS

500g [18oz] white chocolate (this is a large quantity because it is easier to temper; you can remelt and reuse it for another baking project)
orange oil cocoa butter-based food colouring)
OR
150g [5½oz] orange compound chocolate

PLUS

1 quantity of Choux Pastry (see page 134)
½ quantity of Royal Icing (see page 76)
black edible pen or black food dye mixed with a small amount of vodka or alcohol-based extract
edible flowers (if you don't have these, you can cut out flower shapes from the marzipan instead!)
flaked [slivered] almonds or pumpkin seeds

1 / Preheat the oven to 200°C [400°F/Gas mark 6].

2 / Make the orange craquelin. Cream the butter and sugar together in a large bowl until light and fluffy. Add the orange zest and combine. Add the flour and combine with your hands to form a ball. Roll out between 2 sheets of plastic wrap until about 2mm [1/16-in] thick and transfer to the freezer while you make the choux.

3 / Make the choux pastry (see page 134), transfer to a piping bag and cut a medium tip. Pipe 20 x 3-cm

[1¼-in] circles on one baking sheet. Remove the craquelin from the freezer, then cut 20 x 3-cm [1¼-in] circles and place these on top of each choux circle.

4 / Bake for 10 minutes, then reduce the oven to 180°C [350°F/Gas mark 4] and bake for a further 20 minutes. Don't open the oven until at least 25 minutes have passed, to avoid the choux pastry deflating.

5 / While the choux are baking, pipe a second batch onto a second baking sheet. This time you will need 20 x 2-cm [¾-in] circles, and top each with a similarly

sized disc of craquelin (there will be some leftover choux, so you can pipe extra if desired).

6 / When the choux buns have finished baking, immediately turn them over and use a knife to pierce the base. This is so that the air inside has somewhere to escape, and also gives you a place to pipe in the filling. Bake the second batch of choux for 10 minutes at 200°C [400°F/Gas mark 6], then a further 10 minutes at 180°C [350°F/Gas mark 4].

7 / While the choux are baking, make the orange crème diplomate for the filling. Add the milk, orange zest and vanilla bean paste to a medium saucepan. Stir over a low-medium heat until just starting to bubble. Meanwhile, in a separate bowl, whisk the egg yolks and sugar until light and fluffy. Add the cornflour and mix until just combined. When the milk mixture is bubbling, pour a small amount (about a third) into the egg yolk mixture, whisking constantly. When combined, add the rest of the milk while still whisking, then pour it all back into the saucepan.

8 / Put the pan back over a medium heat and whisk by hand until the mixture is very thick. Switch to a spatula when it becomes too thick to whisk, and use the spatula to get right into the edges of the pan. When the mixture is very thick, stir in the orange liqueur and place back on the heat for a few seconds while constantly stirring, to thicken again.

Spoon this crème pâtissière into a shallow metal tray, about 21 x 30cm [8¼ x 12in], or a bowl, cover with plastic wrap (making sure it touches the surface of the crème) and leave to cool in the fridge for 30 minutes. If you have any lumps in your 'crème pat,' you can strain it before chilling.

9 / When the crème pat is completely cool, whip the double cream until it forms soft peaks, then gently fold into the crème. It may help to whisk the crème pat first just to loosen it a bit. With the addition of the whipped cream to lighten it, you now have crème diplomate. Transfer to a piping bag and leave in the fridge until ready to use.

10 / Pipe the crème diplomate into the cooled choux buns through the hole created earlier, making sure each one is filled completely.

11 / Make the marzipan (if using shop-bought marzipan, skip this step). Mix the dry ingredients in a bowl and whisk the wet ingredients, except the food dye, together in a separate bowl. Add the wet to the dry and stir until just starting to combine. Knead on a work surface lightly dusted with icing sugar until it becomes smooth and forms a ball.

12 / Add blue food dye to your marzipan and knead until the colour is evenly distributed. Make the royal icing (see page 76) and transfer to a piping bag.

'Choux can do it!'

13 / On a work surface lightly dusted with icing sugar, roll the marzipan out thinly, about 2mm [¹⁄₁₆-in] and cut out 20 circles, about 6cm [2½-in] in diameter, then place one on top of each larger choux bun, using royal icing to make it stick. Then use royal icing to pipe dots around the border of each marzipan circle. Place the smaller choux bun on top, again using royal icing to make it stick. Use black edible pen or black food dye mixed with a little vodka to draw in eyes and a dot for the mouth (see picture opposite).

14 / Temper the white chocolate (see page 66) and add orange oil or cocoa butter-based food colouring to make it orange, or melt orange compound chocolate and skip the tempering (see page 46). Smooth the chocolate over acetate (or baking paper) and leave to set. Use a cutter to stamp out 2.5–3-cm [1–1¼-in] circles from the chocolate (you

can heat the edge of the cutter with warm water to make it easier). Place a small chocolate circle on top of each choux bun, secured with a little royal icing. Decorate with an edible flower of your choice.

15 / Finally, insert flaked almonds or pumpkin seeds into the sides to create arms.

- LITTLE BAKES -

Pistachio Choux Turtles

You will turtley love making these adorable creatures and the pistachio crème diplomate filling is a dream to bite into.

MAKES: 20–24

CHOUX PASTRY
85g [½ cup plus 2 tsp] unsalted butter
225ml [1 cup] water
pinch of salt
50g [6 Tbsp] plain [all-purpose] flour
50g [5¾ Tbsp] strong white [bread] flour
2–3 medium eggs

CRAQUELIN
75g [⅓ cup] unsalted butter, at room temperature
75g [6 Tbsp] light muscovado [soft brown] sugar
75g [½ cup plus 1 Tbsp] plain [all-purpose] flour

PISTACHIO CREME DIPLOMATE
400ml [1¾ cups] whole milk
¾ tsp vanilla bean paste
7 large egg yolks
110g [½ cup plus 1 Tbsp] caster [superfine] sugar
60g [⅔ cup] cornflour [cornstarch]
2–3 Tbsp pistachio paste (shop-bought)

170ml [¾ cup] double [heavy] cream

PLUS
almond halves
edible black pen or black food dye mixed with a small amount of vodka or alcohol-based extract
edible glitter and edible stars (optional)

1 / Preheat the oven to 200°C [400°F/Gas mark 6]. Line 2 baking sheets with baking paper or a silicone mat.

2 / To make the choux pastry, chop the butter and add it to a small saucepan with the water and salt. Heat until the butter has melted and the mixture is starting to bubble. Meanwhile, combine both flours in a separate bowl. When the butter mixture is bubbling, remove it from the heat and add the flours all in one go. Stir with a wooden spoon until it forms a smooth ball that pulls away from the sides very easily – this is called a panada.

3 / Transfer the panada to a stand mixer (or use a handheld electric whisk) fitted with the paddle attachment and leave to cool for 5–10 minutes.

4 / Meanwhile, make the craquelin for the choux. Cream the butter and sugar together in a large bowl until light and fluffy. Add the flour and combine with your hands to form a ball. Roll out between 2 sheets of plastic wrap and transfer to the freezer.

5 / Add 2 eggs, 1 at a time, to the panada, mixing on slow speed after each addition until combined. Whisk the third egg in a separate bowl and gradually add 1 Tbsp at a time, mixing well after each addition. You are looking for a glossy consistency that leaves a 'v' shape when a spoon is lifted out of the dough.

6 / Transfer to a piping bag and cut a medium tip. Pipe 20 x 3-cm [1¼-in] circles (these will form the body of the turtle), and then pipe a much smaller circles for the head (remember that this will double in size) onto the prepared baking sheets or mat. Insert 4 almond halves per turtle 'body', each one representing a leg. Remove the craquelin from the freezer and cut 20 x 3-cm [1¼-in] circles, then top each choux 'body' with these (see picture on page 136).

7 / Bake for 10 minutes, then reduce the oven to 180°C [350°F/Gas mark 4] and bake for a further 20–25 minutes. Don't open the oven until at least 25 minutes have passed, to avoid the choux deflating. When the buns have finished baking, immediately turn them over and use a knife to pierce the base. This is so that the air inside has somewhere to escape, and also gives you a place to pipe in the filling.

8 / While the choux are baking, make the pistachio crème diplomate for the filling. Put the milk and vanilla bean paste in a medium saucepan and stir over a low-medium heat until just starting to bubble. Meanwhile, in a separate bowl, whisk the egg yolks and sugar until light and fluffy. Add the cornflour and mix until just combined. When the milk mixture is bubbling, pour a small amount (about a third) into the egg yolk mixture, whisking constantly. When combined, add the rest of the milk while still whisking, then pour it all back into the saucepan.

9 / Put the pan back over a medium heat and whisk by hand until the mixture is very thick. Switch to a spatula when it becomes too thick to whisk, and use the spatula to get right into the edges of the pan. When the mixture is very thick, stir in the pistachio paste. Spoon this crème pâtissière into a shallow metal tray, about 21 x 30cm [8¼ x 12in] or a bowl, cover with plastic wrap (making sure it touches the surface of the crème) and leave to cool in the fridge for 30 minutes. If you have any lumps in your 'crème pat', you can strain it before chilling.

10 / When the crème pat is completely cool, whip the double cream until it forms soft peaks, then gently fold into the crème. With the addition of the whipped cream to lighten it, you now have crème diplomate. Transfer to a piping bag and leave in the fridge until ready to use.

11 / Pipe the crème diplomate into the cooled choux buns through the hole created earlier, making sure each one is filled completely.

12 / Finish off by painting each turtles' facial features using an edible black pen or edible black food dye mixed with a little vodka and a paintbrush. You can also sprinkle them with edible glitter and edible stars, if you like.

STEP 6 ▼

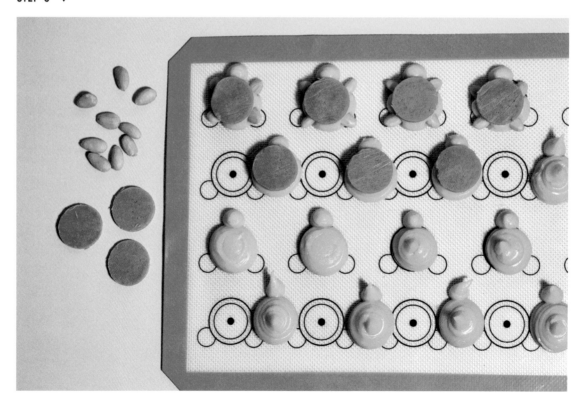

"After you finish making these, you should have a shellebration!'"

Lavender & Lemon Pandaleines

These madeleines are best eaten the same day, and are especially good with a hot cup of tea. The difference in temperature between the hot oven and the cold mixture/pan is what makes these form that distinctive 'hump' that all good madeleines need. And the cute panda faces will add a smile to your face!

> "Don't panda to be what others want. You do you."

MAKES: 12–15

100g [½ cup] caster or granulated sugar
2 medium eggs
70g [⅓ cup minus 1 tsp] salted butter, plus extra for greasing
135g [1 cup] plain [all-purpose] flour

1 tsp baking powder
¾ tsp culinary lavender buds
30ml [2 Tbsp] whole milk

LEMON DIP
40–45ml [2⅔–3 Tbsp] lemon juice

200g [1½ cups minus 1 Tbsp] icing [confectioners'] sugar

PLUS
black food dye
a little extra icing [confectioners'] sugar

1 / Put the caster sugar and eggs, ideally, in a stand mixer (or use a handheld electric whisk) and whisk on high speed for about 7 minutes, or until thick and holds a trail. Meanwhile, melt the butter in 20-second bursts in the microwave so that it is liquid but not too hot. Combine the flour and baking powder in a separate bowl. Grind the lavender with a mortar and pestle to break up.

2 / When the sugar and egg mixture is thick and holds a trail, pour in the milk, then sift in the flour and baking powder. Add the lavender and then whisk until just incorporated. Pour in the cooled melted butter and whisk again until just combined. Do not overmix. Cover with plastic wrap and chill in the freezer for 30 minutes.

3 / Grease a madeleine mould, then freeze it. Preheat the oven to 240°C [475°F/Gas mark 9].

4 / When the mixture has finished chilling, use a spatula to transfer it to a piping bag. Snip a medium tip and pipe 12–15 blobs into the chilled mould.

5 / Place in the oven and immediately reduce the temperature to 200°C [400°F/Gas mark 6]. Bake for 8–12 minutes until each madeleine has a hump and is starting to colour at the edges. When baked, slide them out of the mould and onto a rack.

6 / Meanwhile, make the lemon dip. Whisk the lemon juice and icing sugar together until smooth and runny but still opaque when coating the back of a spoon. Add a little more lemon juice or icing sugar until you have the correct consistency. Pour into a cup suitable for dipping the madeleines into and cover with plastic wrap.

7 / When the madeleines are cool, dip, one by one (narrow, scalloped end first), into the lemon dip. Leave the madeleines to set on a rack.

8 / Mix the remaining lemon dip with black food dye and a little extra icing sugar until it becomes pipeable. Transfer to a piping bag and cut a small tip. When the white icing has set, use the black icing to pipe ears, eyes and a nose on each madeleine.

Farmyard Animal Doughnuts

These doughnuts are clucking adorable and udderly amazing! In fact, you will want to hog them all yourself!

MAKES: ABOUT 7 RING DOUGHNUTS AND 7 ROUND DOUGHNUTS

DAIRY-BASED DOUGH
375g [2⅔ cups] strong white [bread] flour
40g [3¼ Tbsp] caster or granulated sugar
8g [½ Tbsp] salt
10g [⅓oz] fast-action dried [active dry] yeast
grated zest of ½ lemon or ½ orange (optional)
60ml [¼ cup] water
55ml [3⅔ Tbsp] whole milk
3 large eggs
80g [⅓ cup] unsalted butter, at room temperature

VEGAN TANGZHONG PASTE
25g [2¾ Tbsp] strong white [bread] flour
100ml [⅓ cup plus 1 Tbsp] water

VEGAN DOUGH
75ml [5 Tbsp] sunflower or neutral-tasting oil, plus extra for oiling
2 Tbsp aquafaba (see page 30)
90ml [⅓ cup] soy milk
40g [3¼ Tbsp] caster or granulated sugar
8g [½ Tbsp] salt

275g [2 cups] strong white [bread] flour, plus extra for dusting
12g [½oz] fast-action dried [active dry] yeast

GLAZE
200g [1½ cups] icing [confectioners'] sugar
30–40ml [2⅔ Tbsp] lemon juice

FILLING
jam, chocolate spread, ganache (see page 124), curd (see pages 126–127) or Crème Diplomate (see pages 130 and 134)

PLUS
oil, for deep-frying
caster or granulated sugar, for dusting if not going to decorate the doughnuts
black, yellow and orange food dyes
pink gel food dye
about 100g [3½oz] marzipan (either shop-bought or see page 130)
your choice of favourite cookies

Make either the dairy-based dough or the vegan dough following the appropriate method below.

DAIRY-BASED DOUGH

1a / If working by hand, add the flour, sugar, salt, yeast and grated zest, if using, to a large bowl and stir together for a few seconds to distribute the ingredients evenly.

2a / In a separate bowl, whisk the water, milk and eggs together. Add the liquid ingredients to the dry, and use a spoon to combine until you achieve a rough dough. Tip the dough out onto a work surface and knead until smooth and elastic.

3a / Gradually add the butter (40g [3 Tbsp] at a time) and knead in. The dough may stick to the work surface, but it is important to avoid adding any extra flour. Use a dough scraper to clean the work surface as you go along.

1b / If you have a bread machine or stand mixer fitted with a dough hook, simply add all the dry ingredients, stir, then add all the wet ingredients, except the butter. Let the machine knead the dough until smooth and elastic, about 7 minutes, then add the butter and let the machine knead this in for a further 5 minutes.

TANGZHONG VEGAN DOUGH

1 / First, make the tangzhong paste. Using a balloon whisk, mix the flour and water together in a pan until smooth. Switch to a spatula, and continue to stir over a medium heat until thickened to a pudding-like consistency and it has reached 65°C [149°F]. Pour into a bowl, cover with plastic wrap (make sure this touches the surface of the tangzhong) and chill in the freezer for 10 minutes.

2 / Meanwhile, add the oil, aquafaba, soy milk, caster sugar and salt to a large bowl or stand mixer if you have one. Add the chilled tangzhong to the bowl and whisk together (the oil will separate – this is normal and expected), then add the flour and yeast.

3a / If using a stand mixer, just allow the machine to knead the mixture for 10 minutes with the dough hook attachment.

3b / If working by hand, use a wooden spoon to combine everything into a shaggy ball of dough, then turn out onto a floured surface and knead by hand for about 10–15 minutes. The dough will be sticky to start with, but avoid adding too much flour – it will gradually become less sticky as you knead it. If the dough sticks to the surface, use a dough scraper to scrape it off. Keep kneading until the dough is smooth; it will still be a little tacky, but that is normal.

4 / Place the ball of dough into a lightly oiled large bowl and cover with plastic wrap. Leave to rise until doubled in size. This might take around 2–3 hours at room temperature.

You can speed up the rise by placing the covered dough in the oven preheated to a very low temperature (about 30°C [86°F]).

5 / When the dough has risen, knock it back and then roll out on a lightly floured surface until about 8mm [⅓-in] thick. The dough will keep trying to shrink back every time you roll it out, so allow it to relax and shrink back a little, and then roll it out again to get the desired thickness. Make sure the dough is relaxed and not still shrinking back before you start to stamp out the doughnut shapes. This will help you to get even and round shapes. If the dough is still trying to shrink back, then the doughnuts will look misshapen.

6 / Stamp out 7 circles (I use an 8.5-cm [3½-in] diameter cutter) and carefully transfer each of these to an individual square of baking paper. Once transferred, you can then cut out the centres (I use a 4-cm [1½-in] diameter cutter). Removing the centres after transferring to baking paper helps to make sure that each ring doughnut is even in size and shape.

7 / Divide the remaining dough into 7 x 50-g [1¾-oz] pieces. Shape each of these into a smooth ball and try to create a smooth, taut surface so that oil does not get into cracks later and that they puff up evenly in the oil. Press down slightly on each doughnut to flatten. Place each doughnut on a square of baking paper. Loosely cover the doughnuts with lightly oiled plastic wrap.

8 / Leave to rise for about 1–2 hours (depending on room temperature) until doubled in size.

9 / Heat enough oil for deep-frying in a large, deep, heavy-based saucepan to 180–185°C [356°–365°F] and try to maintain this temperature while frying the doughnuts. Fry about 3 doughnuts at a time, carefully lowering them into the oil along with the baking paper underneath (this helps the doughnuts to keep their shape and not deflate during transfer). Use tongs or a similar utensil to remove the baking paper from the oil as quickly as possible. Fry the ring doughnuts for 45 seconds per side, and fry the round doughnuts for 1 minute 40 seconds per side.

10 / When the doughnuts have been fried on both sides, remove from the oil with a slotted spoon and drain on paper towels. After the oil has been soaked up, you can coat these in caster sugar straightaway (they are irresistible when still warm from the pan), or you can decorate them as animals and fill the round doughnuts with your choice of filling!

11 / When the doughnuts have cooled, use a knife to poke a hole in the visible white ring of the round doughnuts. Fill a piping bag with your desired doughnut filling, then pipe this into the hole. You can weigh the doughnuts before and after if you want to know how much filling you are putting in each.

TO DECORATE

Make the glaze by whisking the icing sugar and lemon juice together in a bowl until smooth, then follow the instructions for the animal designs below.

COW DOUGHNUTS

1 / Put a quarter of the glaze in a separate bowl and add a little icing sugar until it is pipeable. Mix with black food dye and then transfer to a piping bag. Cut a small tip.

2 / Dip round doughnuts (no hole) into the white glaze until evenly covered. Use a finger to smooth the icing that tries to drip down the side. Leave for a few minutes to semi-set.

3 / Use the black icing to pipe on black markings of a cow, leaving space for the face in the middle.

4 / Knead a tiny amount of pink gel food dye into marzipan (you can use shop-bought or make it yourself, see page 130) to colour, and then use your fingers to shape the marzipan into the cow's nose and ears. Place these features on the doughnuts.

5 / Finish by using the black icing to pipe the cow's eyes, nostril details and mouth (see picture above).

PIG DOUGHNUTS

1 / Keep the majority of the glaze for dipping, but place a small amount in a separate bowl and add black food dye. Mix in a little extra icing sugar until it is pipeable. Transfer to a piping bag ready for later.

2 / Add a tiny amount of pink gel food dye to the majority of the glaze and then dip ring doughnuts into it until evenly covered. Use a finger to smooth the icing that tries to drip down the side. Leave for a few minutes to semi-set.

3 / Knead a tiny amount of pink gel food dye into marzipan (you can use shop-bought or make it yourself, see page 130) to colour, and then use your fingers to shape the marzipan into the pig's nose and ears. Position these on the doughnut.

4 / Use the black icing to pipe the pig's eyes and nostril details.

5 / Pipe darker pink icing to detail the pig's tail, then position your favourite (half-eaten) cookie over the doughnut hole to look as if the pig is eating it.

6 / Make 2 small round balls out of the marzipan, and position to look like the pig is holding the cookie.

CHICK DOUGHNUTS

1 / Keep the majority of the glaze for dipping, but place a small amount in 3 separate bowls. Add yellow food dye to the main glaze and mix in.

2 / Add orange food dye to one of the small bowls, black to another and pink to the last one. Mix in a little extra icing sugar until they are pipeable. Transfer these to piping bags ready for later.

3 / Dip ring doughnuts into the yellow glaze until evenly covered. Use a finger to smooth the icing that tries to drip down the side. Leave for a few minutes to semi-set.

4 / Pipe the orange icing to detail the feet and nose. Add the eyes using the black icing. Add little pink lines under the eyes.

5 / Position your favourite (half-eaten) cookie over the doughnut hole to look as if the chick is eating it.

6 / Add a litte icing sugar to the main dipping glaze until it is pipeable. Transfer to a piping bag and use to pipe the wings to look like the chick is holding the cookie (see picture below).

Passionfruit & Strawberry Tarts with Cat Meringues

"Sometimes you have a clawful week and then a string of pawsitive things happen!"

Fluffy, white and slightly jiggly meringue cats on these tarts just complete them. Imagine serving these to your friends at a party! They will love them! Have fun creating the cats however you want to. You can do one giant cat if you like or lots of little ones. I've created a family of cats, chilling out on their cosy passionfruit cushion after being tired of playing about – standard cat behaviour.

MAKES: 6 X 10-CM [4-IN] TARTS

PASTRY
180g [1⅓ cups] plain [all-purpose] flour, plus extra for dusting
125g [½ cup plus 1 Tbsp] slightly salted butter, at room temperature
30g [2 Tbsp] caster or granulated sugar
2 Tbsp beaten egg

PASSIONFRUIT CURD
12 passionfruit (all the juice and 1 Tbsp seeds)
110g [½ cup] salted butter
5 large egg yolks
125g [⅔ cup] caster or granulated sugar

ITALIAN MERINGUE
80g [2¾oz] egg white (from about 2–3 eggs)
160g [¾ cup plus 1 Tbsp] caster [superfine] sugar
80ml [⅓ cup] water

PLUS
black food dye
freeze-dried strawberry pieces
strawberry laces or other sweets [candies] (not pictured, but you can add these to look like the cats have been playing with string!)

1 / Grease 6 x 10-cm [4-in] tart tins.

2 / Add the flour to a large bowl. Chop the butter and add to the bowl, then rub the butter into the flour until it resembles fine breadcrumbs. Don't overwork. Stir in the sugar. Make a well, add the beaten egg and beat with a fork, gradually combining it with the rest of the mixture. Use your hands to form the pastry into a ball.

3 / Roll the pastry out on a generously floured surface. Using a 12-cm [4½-in] cutter, stamp out circles to line each of the tart tins. Guide the pastry into the shape of the tart tin. Trim off the top edges and prick the bases a few times with a fork.

4 / Place the tart shells in the fridge for 20 minutes, or the freezer for less time if you're in a rush. Meanwhile, preheat the oven to 200°C [400°F/Gas mark 6].

5 / Cover the tarts with foil, then fill with baking beans [pie weights] (or rice or lentils), making sure they spread into all the edges. Blind bake for 15 minutes, then remove the foil and baking beans and bake for a further 5–10 minutes so that the pastry is golden brown.

6 / While the tarts are baking, make the passionfruit curd. Scoop the passionfruit pulp out and blend in a food processor for just for a few seconds to loosen the seeds. Strain the juice into a pan, then add 1 Tbsp of the passionfruit seeds. Chop the butter, add to the pan and heat over a low heat until it has melted.

7 / In a separate bowl, whisk the egg yolks and sugar together. Pour about a sixth of the hot fruit and butter mix onto the egg yolk mix, whisking constantly, then pour all this back into the pan. Continue whisking over a medium heat until it is thick and holds a trail.

Transfer to a bowl and cover with plastic wrap if the tart shells are not yet out of the oven.

8 / When the tart shells are baked and golden brown, remove from the tart tins and add a generous amount of curd to each.

9 / Now make the Italian meringue. Add the egg whites to a stand mixer (or use a handheld electric whisk). Heat the caster sugar and water in a small saucepan over a medium-high heat, stirring initially but stopping stirring once the sugar has dissolved and the mixture starts bubbling. When the mixture reaches 100°C [212°F], start whisking the egg whites. You want them to reach firm peaks at the same time as the sugar syrup reaches 115°C [239°F]. You can adjust the speed at which you whisk the egg whites to time the two together.

10 / When the sugar syrup reaches 115°C [239°F], pour it down the side of the bowl of whisked egg whites in a thin, steady stream while whisking on maximum speed. Make sure you don't pour the sugar syrup directly onto the whisk, and make sure you keep the mixer on maximum speed to prevent hot sugar splashing on you!

STEP 12 ▼

11 / Whisk for a further 5–10 minutes until the meringue has cooled (the bottom of the bowl will no longer feel hot to the touch), then transfer the meringue to 2 piping bags. Cut a larger tip for one piping bag (this is for piping the bodies and heads of the cats), and cut a smaller tip for the other piping bag (for piping the ears, legs and tails).

12 / Pipe an oval blob for each cat's body, then a round blob for the head on one end of the body (see picture opposite). Dip your finger in a little water and use this to flatten any peaks that form. Use the small piping bag to add the ears, legs and tail, again using water to help shape.

13 / Dip a cocktail stick [toothpick] into a very tiny amount of black food dye (too little is better than too much!), and use to draw in the cats' facial features (see picture above). Make lots of tiny pricks into the meringue to draw the details, rather than dragging the cocktail stick through the meringue.

14 / Finish with a sprinkling of crushed freeze-dried strawberry pieces. You can also use strawberry laces or other spaghetti-like sweet treats so that it looks like the cats are playing with string (not pictured)!

Meringues

Meringues are one of those things that a lot of people view as tricky, but they are straightforward really – they just require patience and following the instructions carefully. The great thing is that when you are confident with meringue, then you can make lots of different creations from it!

MAKES: LOTS OF LITTLE MERINGUES!

MERINGUE

140g [¾ cup minus 2 tsp]
 caster [superfine] sugar
80g [2¾oz] egg whites
pinch of cream of tartar
 (optional)

VEGAN MERINGUE

140g [¾ cup minus 2 tsp]
 caster [superfine] sugar
80g [⅓ cup] aquafaba
 (see page 30)
pinch of cream of tartar
 (optional)

"Every day is a new day. Don't let a single bad day cloud that."

The method for both meringues is essentially the same, the only difference being that the vegan meringues take a little longer to whisk to soft peaks initially, and are best baked until completely dry in the centre. The purpose of putting meringues in the oven is to dry them out rather than cook them, so don't be tempted to turn the oven up higher!

1 / Preheat the oven to 200°C [400°F/Gas mark 6]. Line a baking sheet with baking paper and spread out the caster sugar. Place in the oven for about 7–8 minutes until warm but not caramelized, discarding any bits that are caramelized and replacing with an equal weight of caster sugar. Leave the oven door open to allow it to cool down to 100°C [212°F/Gas mark ¼].

2 / Add the egg whites or aquafaba to a stand mixer (you can use a handheld electric whisk but you will be whisking for a long time, so a stand mixer is ideal). Mix on high speed until you have soft peaks, then gradually add the sugar, 1 Tbsp at a time, whisking for about 30–60 seconds after each addition. It is important to add the sugar very slowly so that it all dissolves properly.

3 / When all the sugar has been incorporated (the meringue mixture should feel smooth and not gritty between your fingers), add the cream of tartar, if using, then use a spatula to transfer the meringue to a piping bag.

4 / Pipe desired meringue shapes onto baking paper or a silicone mat and bake for 45–60 minutes for meringues that are gooey in the centre, or bake for 1 hour 30 minutes, then switch off the oven and leave the oven door closed for a few hours to completely crisp and dry the meringues.

MERINGUE MUSHROOMS

Pipe a meringue 'kiss' (for the mushroom top), then pipe another that's smaller in diameter but taller (for the mushroom stalk). Dip your finger in water and use this to smooth down the tips of the meringue. Bake as normal, then insert the mushroom stalk into the base of the top. You can sift cocoa powder on top to give the mushroom colour and life.

MERINGUE PEOPLE

Turn your meringues into miniature versions of your family and friends! Pipe and bake meringue kisses as normal, then use gel food dye mixed with a little vodka to paint their facial features.

RAINBOW MERINGUE KISSES
You can add gel food dye to the meringue mixture before baking, or you can paint thin stripes of gel food dye in the piping bag before filling with the meringue mixture and then piping. You can experiment with different colours and effects.

MERINGUE SNOWMEN
Pipe a meringue blob, then pipe a smaller meringue blob on top. Dip your finger in water and use this to smooth down the tip of the meringe. Bake as normal, then decorate with royal icing (see page 76).

MERINGUE GHOSTS
Pipe and bake meringue kisses as normal, then use black gel food dye mixed with a little vodka to paint ghoulish faces. You can vary these and create different personalities for your ghosts! If there are any cracks in the meringue, you can be creative and incorporate these into the ghost's expression.

MERINGUE CLOUDS
Pipe 3 interconnected blobs at the bottom, then 2 blobs above, then wet the tip of your finger and use this to press down any peaks that don't look cloud-like. See page 55.

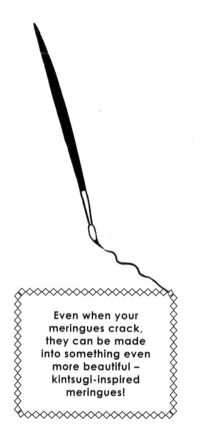

Even when your meringues crack, they can be made into something even more beautiful – kintsugi-inspired meringues!

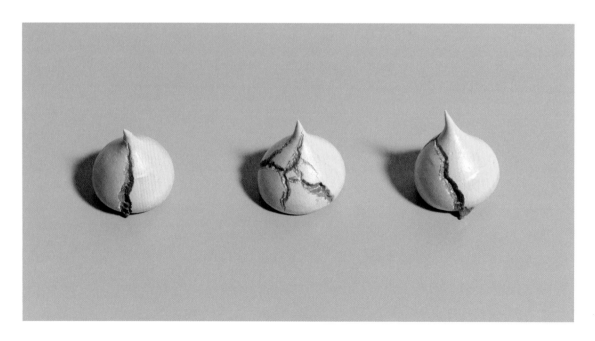

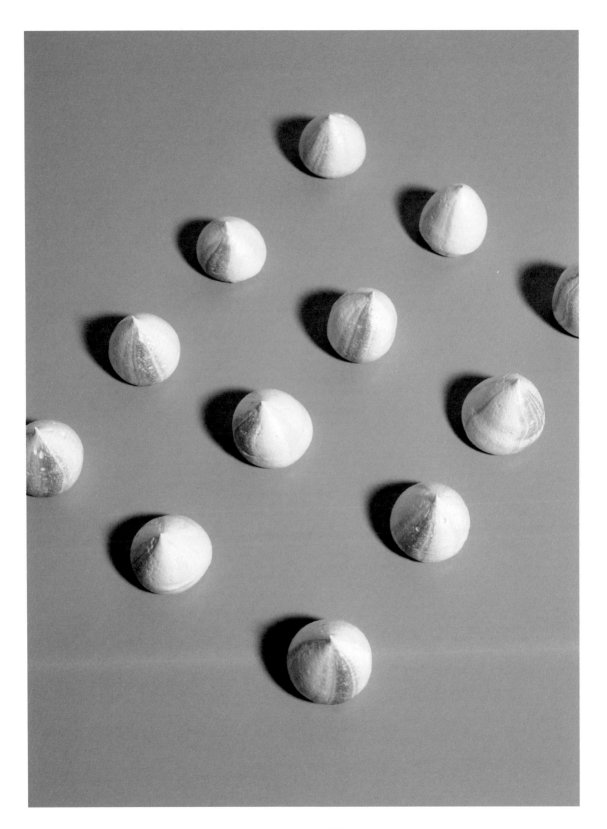

Chocolate & Cherry Bear Madeleines

I'm pleased to be the bearer of good news! Which is that you can make these pretty quickly and they are unbearably cute. Plus because madeleines are so small, you won't be able to resist eating one after another. Enjoy!

MAKES: 12–15

100g [½ cup] caster or granulated sugar
2 medium eggs
70g [⅓ cup minus 1 tsp] salted butter, plus extra for greasing
135g [1 cup] plain [all-purpose] flour
1 tsp baking powder

30ml [2 Tbsp] whole milk
½ tsp vanilla bean paste

KIRSCH SIMPLE SYRUP
40ml [2⅔ Tbsp] water
40g [3¼ Tbsp] caster or granulated sugar
1 Tbsp kirsch, or to taste

PLUS
12–15 frozen cherries
200g [7oz] dark chocolate, broken into pieces (this seems like a lot of chocolate, but you need to have enough so that you can easily dip in the madeleines)

about 50g [1¾oz] white chocolate (or compound chocolate), broken into pieces, plus a few drops of oil/cocoa butter-based white food colouring
about 30g [1oz] blue compound chocolate

1 / Put the caster sugar and eggs in, ideally, a stand mixer (or use a handheld electric whisk) and whisk on high speed for about 7 minutes, or until thick and holds a trail. Meanwhile, melt the butter in 20-second bursts in the microwave so that it is liquid but not too hot. Combine the flour and baking powder in a separate bowl.

2 / When the sugar and egg mixture is thick and holds a trail, pour in the milk, then sift in the flour and baking powder. Add the vanilla bean paste and then whisk until just incorporated. Pour in the cooled melted butter and whisk again until just combined. Do not overmix. Cover with plastic wrap and chill in the freezer for 30 minutes.

3 / Grease a madeleine mould, then freeze it. Preheat the oven to 240°C [475°F/Gas mark 9].

"Paws and take some time out to enjoy these."

4 / While the mixture is chilling, prepare the kirsch simple syrup. Bring the water and caster sugar to a simmer in a saucepan over a medium-high heat. Stir until all the sugar has dissolved, then transfer to a bowl and leave to cool before adding the kirsch.

5 / When the madeleine mixture has finished chilling, use a spatula to transfer it to a piping bag. Snip a medium tip and pipe 12–15 blobs into the chilled mould. You can pipe the mixture into the centre of the mould without worrying about spreading it into the edges – the hot oven will do the work for you! You can use a tablespoon, but I find that piping is actually easier and quicker, and this way you can make sure each madeleine is the same size. Place a frozen cherry on top of each madeleine – you don't need to push it fully into the mixture because it will rise and cover most of the cherry.

6 / Place in the oven and immediately reduce the temperature to 200°C [400°F/Gas mark 6]. Bake for 8–12 minutes until each madeleine has a hump and is starting to colour at the edges.

7 / When the madeleines are baked, slide them out of the mould and onto a rack. Immediately brush them with the kirsch simple syrup.

8 / Melt the dark chocolate in a microwave-safe bowl, using 30-second bursts and stirring well after each burst. Pour into a cup suitable for dipping the madeleines into.

9 / When the madeleines are cool, dip, one by one (narrow, scalloped end first), into the dark chocolate. Leave the madeleines to set on a rack.

10 / You will have leftover melted dark chocolate. Transfer this to a piping bag and cut a small tip. Use this to add ears to each madeleine.

11 / Leave to set while you melt the white chocolate (or compound chocolate). Use 15–30-second bursts in the microwave and stir well after each burst. Add the white oil or cocoa butter-based food colouring to colour if using the white chocolate rather than

compound chocolate. Transfer the melted white chocolate to a piping bag and cut a small tip. Use this to add the white patch for the bear's nose and mouth, then pipe the eyes and add the white detailing on the ears.

12 / Melt the blue compound chocolate (again in short bursts in the microwave), transfer to a piping bag and use this to add the small blue circles for the bear's cheeks.

13 / Use the dark chocolate to add dots for the eyes. For the mouth and nose, you will need to transfer the dark chocolate to a piping bag with a very small tip for very fine lines. It helps to pipe lots of little dots rather than pipe lines that may end up too thick. Leave to set.

Rhubarb & Frangipane Butterfly Tart

Butterflies come out when rhubarb is in season, and so they are sitting on top of this tart to celebrate that it's spring – and telling you that a rhubarb frangipane tart with a crisp pastry shell is just what you need on a warm day. Especially paired with some cream or custard. Bliss.

SERVES: 6–8

ROYAL ICING BUTTERFLIES

(make these the night before so that they have time to set overnight before decorating with)
½ quantity of Royal Icing (see page 76)
blue and pink gel food dyes

PASTRY

225g [1⅔ cups] plain [all-purpose] flour, plus extra for dusting
155g [⅔ cup] salted butter at room temperature, plus extra for greasing
40g [3¼ Tbsp] caster or granulated sugar
2½ Tbsp beaten egg

FRANGIPANE

100g [½ cup] caster or granulated sugar
100g [½ cup minus 1 Tbsp] unsalted butter, at room temperature
1 medium egg
¾ tsp almond extract
100g [1 cup] ground almonds

PLUS

about 3 sticks of rhubarb
honey or apricot jam, to glaze after baking
edible flowers (optional)

1 / To make the royal icing butterflies, make the royal icing (see page 76). Divide among 3 bowls and use food dye to colour one blue and one pink; leave the third white. Transfer to piping bags and cut very small tips.

2 / Draw a butterfly template onto a piece of paper. Fold a rectangular strip of baking paper in half lengthways. Place the butterfly template underneath (with the crease corresponding with the centre of the butterfly) and use this to guide piping the butterfly wing outlines. Fill in each wing, using the white, blue and pink icing colours to create different patterns. Leave for a few minutes to semi-set.

3 / Now pipe white icing along the centres of the butterflies (see picture on page 160). Immediately transfer to a piece of cardboard folded lengthways and propped up in a 'v' shape – this is so that the butterflies set with their wings upwards, rather than flat. Leave to set completely overnight.

4 / When you're ready to start making the tart, grease a 35 x 13-cm [14 x 5-in] rectangular tart tin, preferably fluted.

5 / Add the flour to a large bowl. Chop the butter and add to the bowl, then rub the butter into the flour until it resembles fine breadcrumbs. Don't overwork. Stir in the sugar. Make a well, add the beaten egg and beat with a fork, gradually combining it with the rest of the mixture. Use your hands to form the pastry into a ball.

6 / Roll the pastry out on a well floured surface and roll out to the thickness of a coin. Make sure you roll it out bigger than the tart tin (any leftovers can be kept in the fridge and used for other baking). Lift and drape the pastry over the tin, then use your fingers to tuck the pastry into the edges of the tin. Use the side of a finger to press the pastry into the fluted edges and trim off the top edge (you can press a rolling pin onto the edge of the tin to make this easier).

7 / Chill the tart tin in the fridge for at least 30 minutes, or in the freezer for about 10 minutes if you're in a rush. Meanwhile, preheat the oven to 180°C [350°F/Gas mark 4].

8 / When the pastry is chilled and firm to the touch, cover with foil, pressing into all the edges, then fill completely with baking beans [pie weights] (or rice or lentils), making sure they spread into all the edges. Blind bake for 15 minutes.

9 / Meanwhile, make the frangipane. Cream the sugar and butter together in a stand mixer (or use a handheld electric whisk) on high speed until light and fluffy. Add the egg and almond extract and mix until just combined. Fold in the ground almonds, then set aside for now.

10 / When the pastry has finished blind baking, remove the baking beans and the foil lining and leave to cool completely. Keep the oven on.

11 / Meanwhile, slice each rhubarb stalk down the middle and chop into equal lengths that will fit exactly in the pastry shell.

12 / When the pastry is cool, spoon in the frangipane and level out, then arrange rhubarb pieces on top. Bake for about 25 minutes, or until the frangipane has set.

13 / Immediately after the tart comes out of the oven, brush with honey or apricot jam for shine.

14 / When completely set, lift each butterfly carefully off the paper and position on the tart. Don't try to lift them too soon, as they will break!

You can bake this in other tin shapes, but rectangular tarts are the easiest, as each rhubarb length is equal. It is quite fun to play about with rhubarb shapes in round tart tins, though – a bit like a jigsaw!

STEP 3 ▼

- LITTLE BAKES -

"Spread your wings and fly high."

Jam Love Letters

The pastry for these is very short, so it gives a nice melt-in-your-mouth cookie-like texture. These are so simple to make, but as they are specially made for your loved ones with custom notes, they will really appreciate it.

MAKES: 6–8

STRAWBERRY JAM (OPTIONAL)
500g [4 cups] strawberries
juice of ½ lemon
450g [2¼ cups] jam sugar
you can also add chia seeds for extra texture

PASTRY
180g [1⅓ cups] plain [all-purpose] flour, plus extra for dusting
140g [⅔ cup] unsalted butter
40g [3¼ Tbsp] caster or granulated sugar
1 medium egg yolk

1 egg, lightly beaten, for brushing

OPTIONAL EXTRAS
you can add the grated zest of 1 orange to the pastry for a little extra aciditiy and flavour

ROYAL ICING
½ quantity of Royal Icing (see page 76)
black food dye

1 / For the strawberry jam, if making, wipe the strawberries rather than washing, then cut them into quarters and remove the stem. Add these to a pan along with the lemon juice and sugar. Stir very occasionally over a low heat until the sugar has dissolved. When the sugar has dissolved, turn up the heat and bring the jam to the boil for about 5–10 minutes until it reaches 105°C [221°F]. Skim the foam off the top, then pour into sterilized jars. Leave to cool before using.

2 / Line a baking sheet with baking paper (ideally you want a baking sheet that can fit in your fridge).

3 / Add the flour to a large bowl. Chop the butter and add to the bowl, then rub the butter into the flour until it resembles fine breadcrumbs. Don't overwork. Stir in the sugar. Make a well, add the egg yolk and beat with a fork, gradually combining it with the rest of the mixture. Use your hands to form the pastry into a ball.

4 / Roll the pastry out on a generously floured surface. Use a ruler to mark out and cut 10-cm [4-in] squares. Stamp out 6–8 small flowers or hearts using a plunger cutter or similar.

5 / Place each pastry square in turn in front of you in a diamond shape. Spoon 1 generous tsp of jam into the centre, then fold the left- and right-hand corners of the pastry into the centre. Carefully fold the bottom corner up into the centre, then secure with a dot of beaten egg and a small pastry flower/heart on top. It should now look like an open envelope.

6 / Chill in the fridge for 20 minutes before baking. (If you skip this step, they will still be delicious!)

7 / Preheat the oven to 200°C [400°F/Gas mark 6]. Bake for 15–20 minutes until golden brown.

8 / Leave to cool on the baking sheet for 5–10 minutes before gently transferring to a wire rack to finish cooling.

9 / Make the royal icing and colour it black (see page 76), then transfer to a small piping bag and snip a small tip. When the love letters have completely cooled, use this to pipe lines on the envelope and a little heart.

Mince Pies

These are so delicious because the pastry is buttery while still being easy to handle and shape. There is just a small amount of sugar in the pastry, which helps to offset the sweetness of the filling. Topped with cute reindeers, polar bears, cats, foxes and penguins with antlers, these are extra festive and delightful.

MAKES: 10 MEDIUM AND 10 MINI MINCE PIES

MINCEMEAT (OPTIONAL)
125g [½ cup] butter
3 cooking apples, peeled and finely chopped
200g [1½ cups] currants
200g [1½ cups] sultanas [golden raisins]
200g [1½ cups] raisins
200g [1⅔ cups] dried cranberries
50g [1¾oz] dried cherries, finely chopped
60g [½ cup] pecans, finely chopped
250g [1¼ cups] light muscovado [soft brown] sugar
grated zest and juice of 2 oranges
grated zest of 2 lemons
juice of 1 lemon
4 tsp mixed spice [apple pie spice]
1 tsp ground cinnamon
¼ tsp ground nutmeg
150ml [⅔ cup] brandy

PASTRY
365g [2¾ cups] plain [all-purpose] flour
250g [1 cup plus 2 Tbsp] slightly salted butter, at room temperature, plus extra for greasing
60g [5 Tbsp] caster or granulated sugar
2 medium eggs

ROYAL ICING
1 quantity of Royal Icing (see page 76)
red, orange, black, pink and grey food dye

1 / For the mincemeat, if making, melt the butter in a large saucepan over a low heat and add all the ingredients, except for the brandy. Bring to a slow simmer and cook, stirring occasionally, for about 10 minutes, or until the apples are soft. Leave to cool completely, then add the brandy. Stir, then transfer to sterilized jars.

2 / Preheat the oven to 220°C [425°F/Gas mark 7]. Grease a 12-hole cupcake tray and 12-hole mini cupcake tray.

3 / Add the flour to a large bowl. Chop the butter and add to the bowl, then rub the butter into the flour until it resembles fine breadcrumbs. Stir in the sugar. Make a well, add one of the eggs and beat with a fork, gradually combining it with the rest of the mixture. Use your hands to form the pastry into a ball, then roll it out on a well-floured surface. Stamp out circles for the bases and tops of the mince pies.

4 / Gently press the larger circles into the cupcake tray and fill about two-thirds with mincemeat.

5 / Lightly beat the remaining egg in a bowl. Use your finger to wet the top edge of the pastry, and place the smaller pastry circle on top. Use your fingers to press this down and ensure that the mincemeat is sealed in, then brush the top with the beaten egg. The process is the same for the smaller mince pies – just use smaller circles relative to the smaller tray.

6 / Bake for 15–20 minutes until golden brown. Leave to cool in the trays for 10 minutes before sliding each pie out. Leave on a rack to finish cooling.

7 / Make the royal icing (see page 76). Distribute the icing between 6 bowls. Leave one bowl white, then dye the others the following colours: red, orange, black, pink and grey. Transfer to small piping bags and snip small tips. Use these to pipe the face of a reindeer, penguins, cats, bears and foxes (and antlers!) onto the pies. Or just pick your favourite animals and decorate all the mince pies with that (just adjust the icing colours you need accordingly).

8 / When set, serve with cream or brandy butter.

Pigfiteroles in Mud

The beauty of these piggies in chocolate is that they are so quick and actually so simple to make, and they taste like chocolate and strawberry dreams wrapped up in a cute pig choux parcel! You can also make these for friends and family and get them to drizzle the chocolate on themselves! Kids and adults alike would love it. And everyone will want to hog them all to themselves!

MAKES: ABOUT 15

STRAWBERRY FILLING
300ml [1¼ cups] double [heavy] cream
2 Tbsp icing [confectioners'] sugar
4 tsp freeze-dried strawberry powder
pink gel food dye

BLACK ROYAL ICING
(this makes more than you need, as it is difficult to make very small quantities, but you can use this on other baking projects!)
½ quantity of Royal Icing (see page 76)
gel black food dye

PLUS
1 quantity of Choux Pastry (see page 134)
about 30g [1oz] marzipan (shop-bought, or make your own, see page 130)
pink gel food dye
dark chocolate, for the mud

"You're an interesting porcine, never a boar!"

1 / Preheat the oven to 200°C [400°F/Gas mark 6]. Line a baking sheet with baking paper or a silicone mat.

2 / Make the choux pastry (see page 134), transfer to a piping bag and cut a medium tip. Pipe about 15 circles onto the prepared baking sheet or mat. Dip your finger in water and use to flatten the tip of the choux.

3 / Bake for 10 minutes, then reduce the oven to 180°C [350°F/Gas mark 4] and bake for a further 20 minutes. Don't open the oven until at least 25 minutes have passed, to avoid the choux pastry deflating.

4 / When the choux buns have finished baking, immediately turn them over and use a knife to pierce the base. This is so that the air inside has somewhere to escape.

5 / While the choux are cooling, make the strawberry filling. Put the cream, sugar and strawberry powder in a clean, grease-free bowl. Whip on medium-high

speed until stiff enough to pipe and hold its shape, but be careful not to overwhip. While whipping, gradually add very small amounts of pink food dye until a pale pink is achieved. Transfer to a piping bag and cut a large tip. Cut the tops off each choux bun, pipe in the whipped cream and replace the top.

6 / Knead a tiny amount of pink food dye into the marzipan. Shape it into noses for the pig faces and place on the whipped cream.

7 / Make the royal icing and dye black (see page 76). Transfer to a piping bag and cut a small tip. Use to pipe each pig's eyes and 2 dots for nostrils.

8 / Melt some dark chocolate in a heatproof bowl set over a pan of gently simmering water. Make sure the bottom of the bowl doesn't touch the water. Arrange the pigfiteroles in a mud bath of melted chocolate and carefully drizzle some chocolate over the tops to finish off your pigfiterole scene! It's best to eat these delicious cuties straightaway... not that that will be difficult at all!

Orange, Cardamom & Salted Caramel Dipping Pot

This makes a great party centrepiece, as everyone can enjoy the fun of dunking their own shortbread dippers into a super-cute edible pot! You can create different faces on the dippers to represent your favourite (or not so favourite!) people. And have the satisfaction of covering them in smooth caramel sauce and biting off their head!

SERVES: 6–8

SHORTBREAD
Semolina Shortbread (see page 74) or Basic Vegan Shortbread (see page 75)
grated zest of 1 orange
1¼ tsp ground cardamom (for the best flavour, finely grind the seeds in a spice grinder)

SALTED CARAMEL DIP
(or you can use any other filling you want, such as your favourite shop-bought spread)
90ml [⅓ cup] water
240g [1⅓ cups] caster or granulated sugar
215ml [1 scant cup] double [heavy] cream
salt, to taste

PLUS
½ quantity of Royal Icing (see page 76)
orange, pink and black food dyes

white fondant (about 30g [1oz]) and edible sprinkles (optional)

1 / Line a baking sheet with baking paper.

2 / Make the shortbread dough (see pages 74 or 75), adding the grated orange zest and ground cardamom to the butter and sugar mixture for the semolina shortbread, and adding it along with the flour for the vegan shortbread.

3 / Roll out the shortbread dough on a lightly floured surface to about 3mm [⅛-in] thick.

4 / Draw these templates onto card: 7 x 6.5cm [2¾ x 2½in] (front/back panels); 7 x 5cm [2¾ x 2in] (side panels); 6.5 x 6.5cm [2½ x 2½in] (base panel); and 1.5 x 1.5cm [⅝ x ⅝-in] (feet panels). Lay the templates on the cookie dough and cut out 4 front/back panels, adding ears to just one; 2 side panes; 1 base panel; and 4 feet. Transfer them to the prepared baking sheet.

5 / Cut the remaining dough into strips about 2 x 7¼cm [¾ x 3in] and transfer to the baking sheet. Chill the dough for 15–30 minutes while you preheat the oven to 160°C [325°F/Gas mark 3].

6 / While the dough is chilling, make the salted caramel dip. Heat the water and sugar in a pan over a low-medium heat, stirring occasionally, until the sugar has fully dissolved. Once the sugar has dissolved, do not stir any more, turn the heat up and wait until the sugar turns an amber colour. You can swill the pan around to even out the colour if you like. Put the cream in a separate small bowl.

7 / When the sugar syrup has turned a deep amber colour, remove the pan from the heat and add all the cream in one go. Stir constantly with a balloon whisk. The sauce will bubble up, so be careful! Return the pan to the stove over a low heat and continue stirring until all the sugar has dissolved and you have

a smooth and creamy sauce. Pour the sauce into a medium bowl and sprinkle with a little salt to taste. Cover with plastic wrap and chill in the freezer for 30–45 minutes. It will thicken as it cools.

8 / Bake the shortbread for 10–15 minutes until just lightly browned at the edges. Leave to cool for 10 minutes on the baking sheet, then gently transfer to a rack to finish cooling.

9 / Meanwhile, make the royal icing (see page 76). Dye the icing as follows: half orange, 2 Tbsp pale pink 2 Tbsp black and leave one-quarter white. Transfer to individual piping bags.

10 / When the shortbread has cooled, use the white icing to stick together the different parts of the dipping pot. Assemble the front (panel with ears) with the sides, then attach the back, and finally attach to the base. Leave to set until totally secure before adding the feet.

11 / Once the box is secure, pipe the details onto the front. Pipe the white and orange background and leave to semi-set.

12 / Now add the pink details and facial details (see pages 78–81 for tips on royal icing decoration). You can also roll out the white fondant and stamp out little flowers to attach to the icing once it has set.

13 / Add little faces to the shortbread dippers!

14 / When the icing on the box is completely set, fill it with the salted caramel dip, decorate with edible sprinkles, if you like, and serve!

There are endless possibilities with this bake! You can try different animal designs for the front of the pot, and maybe create your own shapes and templates. You can also completely change the theme and make it suitable for Halloween, Valentine's Day or Christmas! You don't even have to fill the pot with a dip – you could fill it with layers of delicious pudding or chocolate spread instead.

- LITTLE BAKES -

INDEX

Acknowledgements

This book wouldn't exist if it weren't for all these people who have shaped me in some way, supported me or helped directly with the book.

First, I want to say thank you to Nabil, my partner and best friend – you're always there to listen to me when I am mumbling about whether a cake would look better or worse with an extra cat. Even though your answer is always 'Whatever you think is best', I love that because I always know you have complete faith in me. Not to mention that you are my Number One food taster!

To my mum: thank you for always encouraging me not to just follow the crowd. This is the worst thing to be told when you are 12, but the best thing when you're an adult. And also thank you to Lydia for believing I was going to be an author or to do something special ever since I was small. And thank you to Auntie Audrey, Auntie Sandra, Uncle Yan Teo, Kenneth (though have you even watched the last few episodes of *Bake Off*?), Kevan, Crystal, Julian and the rest of my family around the world.

To the whole team at Quadrille – you have been incredible. Special mentions to Céline Hughes for being a total star and believing in me. Also Maeve Bargman, thank you for being so positive all the time, and for designing a beautiful book. And to Ellis Parrinder for being a friend and taking incredible photos. And to Sarah Hardy for being the best kitchen buddy EVER, and Charlotte Love for all your LOVEly prop work. You all have been a joy to work with (though it didn't feel like work!) and the best team members I could ask for.

Thank you to Vivienne Clore for helping me to navigate the post-*Bake Off* world.

To my friends EJ, JJ, Siân, Charlotte and Simon: I don't know where I'd be without you all! EJ – if we hadn't met under that fan in a club, who knows where I'd be right now! Simon and Charlotte – I'm thankful for you occasionally taking me out of my baking world by chatting to me about *Drag Race*, cats, fashion, music and other important things.

And I am indebted to everyone at Love Productions who gave me the opportunity to be on the *Bake Off* and opened up my world. And thank you to all my *Bake Off* family and friends I've met through baking.

I am also grateful to Linda van den Berg (what beautiful illustrations!), Danni Hooker (for my lovely hair and make-up!), Mary Kate McDevitt (for the lovely title lettering!) and the crew at Travelling Man.

Also thanks to Aaron Copping, Abigail Jill Harding, Adam White, Alicia Hazzard, Amy Bellwood, Anna Appleby, Biserka Stringer-Horne, Chip and Kim, Diane and Len Marlow, Esther Miglio, Holly Homsi, Ian Salmon, Ivan Salazar, Lisa, Darren and Iona, Martha and Gloria, Mark and Jenny, Matt Taylor, Rick Meeson, Richard Starkings, Sarah and Alan, Sarah and Chris, Steve Emmott and all the James family: Pippa, Sammie, Paul and Andrea.

And to everyone who has ever said something kind or positive to me, or taught me something new – thank you. I am beyond grateful to all of you who have made this book a reality.

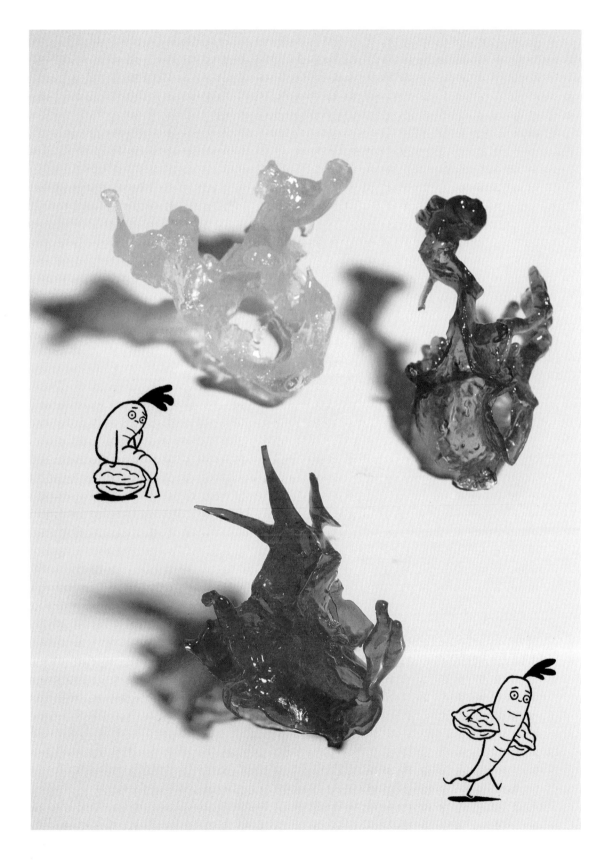

PUBLISHING DIRECTOR: Sarah Lavelle
SENIOR COMMISSIONING EDITOR: Céline Hughes
SENIOR DESIGNER: Maeve Bargman
PHOTOGRAPHER: Ellis Parrinder
ASSISTANT FOOD STYLIST: Sarah Hardy
PROP STYLIST: Charlotte Love
HAIR & MAKE-UP: Danni Hooker
PRODUCTION DIRECTOR: Vincent Smith
PRODUCTION CONTROLLER: Katie Jarvis

Published in 2019 by Quadrille,
an imprint of Hardie Grant Publishing

QUADRILLE
52–54 Southwark Street
London SE1 1UN
quadrille.com

Cataloguing in Publication Data: a catalogue record for this book
is available from the British Library.

ISBN 978 1 78713 458 4

Printed in China